M

A book o̶~ ̶,̶ ̶,̶ ~ prose and short stories

Joella Daniela

ISBN: 1495345254
ISBN-13: 978-1495345258

To my dearest Uncle Moe,
I question a God that would take away someone
that the world needs. I try to have faith that there is a plan
and that you are watching over me.

Love your *little girl*

TABLE OF CONTENTS

I don't know what you do when I'm not around all I know is

ACKNOWLEDGMENTS

I want to thank my mother, Daniela; the most influential woman in my life and I love her more than anything else. She spoils me with love, wisdom and her support has carried me to every stepping stone of my life. I don't know where I would have been if not for her presence.

Also thanks to my truest friend, Zach; from the beginning there was a spark he set off inside of me and it never stops burning.

Lastly, I feel the need to thank every soul I've met on my journey and all those who have read my inner most thoughts. I think about you all often and the ones still present in my life – I treasure you, dearly. You are all in the lines on these pages just as much as you are in my hearts. I hope you can read some of my words and see yourselves in them.

And thank you to my talented cover editor and friend, M.H Freeman, author of *Before I Leave*.

THE REASONS

I write a lot. Writing is therapeutic to me. It's been a place to turn when I was alone and found myself seeking out someone to listen. My pieces whether fictional or fact are confessions of all the me's I know. I use to struggle with what to call myself. I struggled with knowing who I was, and then being afraid of people rejecting that person but I'm breaking free of that.

I believe I am not to be forgotten, not ever. I am superior to no one, only to peoples expectations of me. I'm my own spirit guide. My own faith. My own motivation. I am blessed with infinite talents but finite opportunities to discover them. I will never stop searching.

Sorry to the hearts I broke along the way and perhaps the ones to come.

To my family: I am experiencing life, exploring the world; the one we share and the one within my mind. The tales I tell I gather from both realities. Sorry in advance for the things you will not believe left my lips, but only that it took this long.

"If you end up with a boring miserable life because you listened to your mom, your dad, your teacher, your priest, or some guy on television telling you how to do your shit, then you deserve it."
— **Frank Zappa**

ROMANTICISM

I LOVE

I love... your thoughts, your knots, your kinks and flaws and the way you pause between points. The way your mind is double-jointed like you think this but understand that; and I love how you don't turn your back on your friends. I love how you don't pretend — you just say what you mean and what you meant. I love how you're real, you feel; and even though you're reluctant and you wanna act like you don't hurt sometimes, if I asked I know you'd look me in the eyes and say, *yeah*. I get depressed sometimes. You don't let your pride choke you on the way down when you swallow it. You understand values — none of that hollow shit. You breathe in life and you exhale knowledge. You are forever learning even if you don't agree with college — and I love that. You're an educated — and I don't like this word, but — nigguh, and you shoot off wisdom like your tongue's a trigger. You are the epitome of a man; a guy who treats his girl sweet, his momma like a queen, and takes his grandmama to the movies. You're family-oriented and a good big brother and aren't the type to stack up babymothers, a guy that thinks before he speaks and when he does he can make a girl's knees weak. I've always believed in you, and you believed in me, and nothing is truer than a man who encourages a girl to succeed even without wetting his beak a little — no matter how brittle or easy a riddle it would be to trick me into giving you anything you need. You put me first. You gave me such a thirst to never give up and to always be better, and whatever happened you kept that in my mind and I rewind it all the time. You said I had worth and that I was so cute that it hurt (I may be paraphrasing) but, you made me feel like if no one has I'd probably be the first to change ignorant ways of thinking without blinking. You make me laugh until my ribs feel like they're about to crack — I can't get enough of that. Now, thinking back, you're one of the only real friends I've ever had. It's sad because I'm on the west and you're on the east and we've been friends since we were about fifteen and still never met — and that's absurd, to say the least. But we feasted on each other's minds and spent our late nights and early mornings online, and we always found the time. We roamed different streets, we slept in our own sheets, but we had a world together and I'll remember it forever. Like everything down to how you laughed at the weather here when we were getting snow before winter, and you were over there getting splinters from lawn chairs. I never thought it was fair, but you made it easy to laugh at. You were the bright side of everything and you were all I could ask for had I wanted you to begin with. But, you became the only one who I wanted to sin with. We were like peas in a pod and I swear to god you didn't leave my mind for more than moments at a time. I loved damn near everything about you — even the way you taunted me — because you flaunted me, and everything I never knew was bottled up in your personality, and you challenged me. And now I can finally understand that statement about life, and how friends are either for a season, a reason, a lesson or a blessing — and you were each one.

STUPIDLY IN LOVE

I want to be madly and hopelessly in love; for writing purposes only. I want to write about how they're the first thing that crosses my mind when I open my eyes. I want to write about how I woke up with my phone at my ear to still hear them snoring on the other end.

I want to write about how my mind is consumed with thoughts of them all day and how I doodle their name in my notebook. I want to write about how my day isn't complete until I see them. I want to write about how I know I'm going to marry them, have 4 kids and live in a big house that our love makes a home.

Mostly, I want to write about how their eyes look into my soul and I can't breathe, can't eat, can't sleep because I am so in love. I want to write about how their love confuses me, excites me, explores me, and how I am so tangled up in their presence that I forget where I am, and who I am. I want to write about how excruciatingly happy I am with them.

But I know if I fall in love, the fear of them falling out could be the consequence. Though, I guess I need to experience heartbreak too; for writing purposes.

I'm your instrument; play me

You play the strings
among the things
inside me
and they ring out a tune
in a song – that I can't sing
because
you've taken my breath
     – a long way
from the space
between my lips
never used
to say things on time
only quiet *goodbyes*,
and mumbled, *I wish you would stay's*

You strum me as you hum
play a riff – until,
I'm not stiff in your arms anymore
you hear me echo
I'm so hollow, I'm *hole*
but in your arms as you fill me
with song –
I'm a whole lot better than before

I KEEP THINKING ABOUT WHAT
IT WILL BE LIKE MAKING LOVE TO YOU

Just the thought of you kissing me sends chills up my spine. Goosebumps wrap around my neck like a scarf and subtly creep up my cheeks that turn red. I feel like my thoughts are on the outside of my skin. Skin that will eventually be yours to touch, to hold, to taint. To trail with nimble fingers along the definition of my rising and falling ribcage. Just beneath it enclosed with a heart that belongs to you. That beats for you. That I imagine would begin to race before it stopped all together. Maybe your lips will place weightless kisses on the brink of my chest, up my neck and then devoutly on my parted lips. Lips that I in-exhale through softly as my nerves make me immobile. Maybe I will look at the way your eager eyes trace over my body with the intent to please me. With the intent to do to me, things I don't even know exist. You'll give me a look that asks if I'm ready. I won't be, but I'll nod. You'll touch me where the fluidity of my thoughts escape. You'll smile when you feel the way you affect me. The way you always will. When it's all begun and we are connected the way that we all wish making love would be, we wont take our eyes off of each other. We will be too scared to feel what it will be like to be apart again because nothing feels better than being as close as we are right now. The thoughts will consume us and we will fall into each others skin; with the taste of love and lust and trust on our tongues. Tongues that can't quite express the ecstasy of being in each others company.

I just think
if that person can make you smile once,
can cause you to think twice,
and knows that you aren't perfect
but see's you perfectly –

then you should probably hold onto them.

When I'm with you,
I'm not the person I normally hate.

I WANT YOU

I want you, in everything you are and everything you are not. I want you in your insecurity, in wishing; what you were and what you had. In being blissfully unaware that you are much better than all of that. I want you, when you feel you are failing, when you have lost hope that you are capable of achieving your dreams. I want you, when you are crying. I want you, when you are laughing. I want you when you want me, and even when you don't. I want you when you sleep and when you snore obnoxiously. I want you when you need me to be the thing that makes sense. I want you when you hate yourself so I can show you love. I want you, when you're mad, sad, tired, silly, sappy, lost, useless, cold, with anything, with everything you've got. I want you, in everything you are and everything you're not.

KNIGHTS WITHOUT STARS

Oh, how long I've wondered
when you would find me
in this cavern of the world
I've long awaited
your armour to deflect the flames,
since I was but a girl
Nothing have a dreamed of
more than this —
and I swear it, it is true;
I've awaken to many nights
and knights, and tonight
I'm glad to awake to you

MOONLIT CONFESSIONS

I fell
for you
during a full
moon, it's true-self
came out and
mine did too. I found
sanity that night
in your embrace
sanity in the
expression
across
your
face –

When we
kissed
when
fireworks
sparked
our lips

☾

our eyes were
locked in a glance
and our hearts begun
to dance

And
disappeared
into the wind
as though the
soul of us escaped
our skin. It was then
as the full moon
hung above
you, that
that night,
I knew
I loved
you.

"I LOVE YOU"

He said.

She shoveled a fork full of lasagna in her mouth; emptying her plate as she tried not to let herself fall apart any sooner. Nothing was more pitiful than crying hysterically with a mouthful of food. She swallowed a bite much too big for her liking and downed a glass of water before pushing herself out from the table and disappearing down the hall.

He watched her helplessly not knowing how to respond. Slowly he stood up and cleared both of their plates although his was untouched. He dumped out the food and he placed the dishes in the sink and leaned over the counter beginning to ball and loosen his fists. In a fit of rage he threw everything off the counter and charged his fist into the fridge.

Through the walls she could hear his overactive temper at work. Although, she wasn't sure it was misplaced this time. Her tears bled through her lids as she rocked back and forth in an upward fetal position. Her hands muffing her ears. *Why does this happen to me?* She muttered beneath her breath. *Everything was fine the way it was.*

She could never explain why she felt pain when someone cared for her, especially when she felt just as much pain when no one did. *How could he love me?* She said barely audible. *Look at me. I've locked myself in this room, because of what?* Her thoughts became a rave in her head and nothing would make the noise simmer down. Nothing until a sharp shock jumped through her and she spiraled into an epileptic episode.

Her body quaked, she was without control and she fell to the floor and took the end table down with her.

"*Liv?*" He called as he stopped his rampage in the kitchen, "Liv. You okay?"

He bolted into the room and found her shaking body on the floor and dived towards her; tending to her as he had routinely. He held her until she returned. These moments scared him, when all recognizable emotion was wiped from her face. Even long after her seizure had stopped.

He ran his fingers through her hair, and pulled the blanket from the bed to cover them as he settled on the floor. She felt his comforting touch, still confused why he loved her. But grateful he happened to her. It was then as she was cradled shaking in his arms, she realized he was the one who always brought her back.

HOLD ME

I want to be held by you,
just once.
I want you to feel
how my heart races.
I want you to hold
the skin that has
your name
written all over it.
I want you to grasp me
tight enough, so that
I don't fall apart.
I want you to see
you're the only one
I've ever loved

ELECTROLOVE

I'm in a relationship with my electronics. I see your words so much, I sometimes forget what you look like. I see you in letters and shapes, and the way I write your name. I see you with a blurred face and if I had to pick you out of a crowd I'd expect you to be 2 dimensional in bad blinding lighting, like the crappy camera on your phone.

I carry around my devices to make my world with you to continue to go round and I've become so dependent on things that ground me. I don't like lying down with you, in the palm of my hand, as I wait for you to respond with idle thumbs. I hate asking you 'what if'.. 'What if I did this, what if I did that?' 'What if you were here, *right now* – what would you do?'

I hate having to show you pictures to share my life with you. I spend more time uploading pictures than I do appreciating the moments I spent in them. I spend more time wondering what my life would be like if I was spending it with you, than actually building a relationship together.

I'm completely stunned when I touch other human beings to discover they're not made of metal, plastic or gorilla glass. I'm in a relationship with my electronics. I've begun to think my name is the tone of my texts, because those are my cue.

It drives me insane, yet, each time my electronics die, each time I have no service. I do all I can to get it back, as though it makes you anymore here. As though the drive to insanity is okay because when I take the scenic route, it's all about forgetting you're not here, and forgetting when I close my eyes to imagine your touch it's only in my mind. Forgetting that the sun seems closer to me than you do.

It's all about forgetting to remember 'we' wouldn't exist without out our electronics. And each day I'm forgetting more who I was before I sent my first text.

WHEN YOU SMILE AND IT'S BECAUSE OF ME

When there's a smile on your face
and I'm the one who put it there
I feel like a proud mother watching her child,
who just eighteen years ago could hardly stand
and now they walk the stage at graduation

When you smile and you dry your tears
It feels like I ended the war inside of you
When you smile
and when your eyes are smiling too
I feel like you finally get that you matter

When I can get you to smile,
and laugh until you pee
When I get you to smile that way,
and it's all because of me –

I feel better too.

YOUR LIPS TOLD ME MORE THAN YOU DID

You kiss me like you're making love to me in your mind,
but when I remove my clothes it's like you're not into my kind.

My tongue explores your mouth, like it's tasting every word
tracing along thoughts that went south like the birds
You swallow all your feelings, especially the ones that ache
I can feel the reluctance – I can see it on your face.
Oh, you're a dying breed; there are very few like you
every breath, every step you take is a miracle or two

Your scent makes sense to senses, but not really to me;
Indian Night Jasmine and a distinct aroma of dying dreams
When you pause and the thudding in your chest implodes
I can feel you questioning, if this is how love goes
Fear consumes you, you can see it through your skin
goosebumps making mountains, inhales caving in your ribs

I want to be of comfort, where you can lay your soul at ease
my chest will hold safe keeping, our kiss can be the keys
But when you kiss me, and we're together in your mind
go out on a lark and live it for real this time

LOVING YOU BECAME AN ART

Unrequited love was my medium
my sleeve was my canvas
and I spent forever trying to spell out
the emotions I felt;
whether they be painted, etched, sketched
or sewn into my flesh.

You were a kaleidoscopic array of eccentric prose
that I couldn't quite learn how to mold
I begun to think that,
loving you was easier through the acrylics,
charcoal, watercolor and their hydrophilic pages
that I used to create a portrayal that might —
        show you what loving you is like.

LOVE ME

Love me so hard our rapidly pumping ribs collide our bones until they crush, until they crumble into dust. Love me so good I forget how nothing else feels as it should. Love me so strong we carry the earth in our palms. Love me so true I understand the madness that is Shakespeare, but I will not bid you adieu. Love me so real I am paralyzed by the way you make me feel. Love me so tangled our admiration entwines with love, lust, and all the fine lines of passion. Love me irrationally, passionately, 'til our love flourishes miraculously. Love me so fucking lovely, teach me to know nothing else; and, mostly, enroll me into loving myself.

How to Forget a Writer:

Rinse their words off of your tongue,
as they tasted too good to be true.
Scrub your skin —
where they touched you with ideas.
Forget that they touched you,
forget that they wrote about you,
each chapter, prose, every free verse stanza
exposing a side of you, you thought you hid well

But they're a writer,
and they write about things they know, and
who knows better to be an outsider
in their own skin if it's not worn right.
Only a writer could fully accept you
despite all your annoying habits
and understand how when you scream,
Go away,
that you really mean:
I need you to hold me, but I am too proud to ask
They'll see through your odd behavior,
they'll document it.
They'll turn you into a
Harry Potter, a Catcher in the Rye,
A War and Peace, a Great Gatsby,
A Lord of the Rings or a Da Vinci Code
They'd turn you, in your purest form,
into best sellers — into art
They'd choke back tears as they saw the world
        fall in love with you too.

So, if you want to forget a writer,
forget that they knew you better than you did, yourself
forget the night under the moons watchful gaze,
when you laid in their arms and they broke the silence
as dawn broke the horizon and said:
'You have 173 freckles on this arm. *Hm,* 173.'
like it was nothing at all
like they did not spend the last several moments
counting the scars of your skin,
that they described as stars.

Forget they loved you unclothed,
forget the words that left their tongue in your honor
as they admired you for all you were worth.
Forget the mental stimulation as
they were inside you, or you were inside them
and they were writing a poem along your skin
in their head, as they hold you in the highest regard;
as they decided then, to never forget a thing about you
to never forget an ode to you
to never forget a feeling you made them feel,
to never forget a single smile, a single *freckle*
or a single breath you had ever taken

So if you really want to forget a writer —
one you love no-less — well you can try
or perhaps, never meet one at all.

BREATHE ME

I breathe differently
when you're around
slower,
shallow.
I feel if I breathe
too deeply
I'll lose what life
I have left
You take my breath away,
and you catch me
when I fall;
when you're around,
it's kinda like
I don't breathe at all

I need to be with someone who reads. Someone who is intrigued by language and vocabulary and the empowerment and personas that words can create. Someone who challenges me. Someone who understands me. Someone who pushes me to test my boundaries and someone who believes I will succeed in anything I set my mind to. Someone who gets why I do what I do, and that I'm just trying to keep sane.

I need to be with someone who would put me in my place had I tried to sleep with them the first day. Understanding that the mental and sexual intricacies are both equal but one should come first and then they can come together. Someone who I can have the night with who stimulates my mind. Who tells me about his childhood and why he likes a certain type of woman that doesn't necessarily describe me but rather expands what he's in to. Someone I can vent to completely by accident because I'm so comfortable in his company he became the pages of my diary I pour my heart onto.

We'd laugh. We'd cry when the conversation got deep enough. We'd be soul-mates. We'd do anything that made us happy. Then we'd make love. It'd be okay because he'd treat me as I deserved.

WITHIN YOU

I'm lost, in your eyes,
aren't I?
I'm all you see, when they open
and I'll be all you think of
if you say goodbye,
aren't I?

I'm lost, in your heart,
aren't I?
I swim purposelessly through you
and the waves are divine,
but I was wrong
to leave you loving me,
wasn't I?

COFFEE BEAN

Natural,
integrated into grinds,
waiting to bleed
something
that gives energy and strength,
comfort
but is addictive,
has a distinct aroma,
tastes good with sweets
but stains your teeth

Something,
better in moderation,
because an overdose
is lethal,
and
much like the stains,
stay with you forever.

Whether you want it to,
       or not.

You were once
a coffee bean —
and now you are my drug.

It wasn't until 7AM that I noticed we stayed up all night talking. The light from my computer seemed to counteract the sunlight that begged for my attention through my curtains; I hadn't noticed dawn turn into day. I came to this discovery between a laugh that you had imposed on me for the millionth time since we began speaking. You consumed me. You were all I thought I needed – I was right.

I KNOW, AND YOU KNOW

I am chained to you
I am, you are
We are

There is no safe distance
I cannot get quite,
Far — enough.

You are, I am,
We are as real, as deep
As one may go

We are, you are, I am
Convinced this is it
I know, and you know — too.

FOR LONG DISTANCE LOVERS

I want to make you a quilt. I want to stitch the seams of our memories because I think they fit together quite beautifully. On lonely nights, when I can't be there, I want the threads of those times to be draped over your body to comfort you; the same way I wish I could from a million miles away. I want it to catch the tears you cry on the days you miss me, until I can give you my shoulder. I want you to see that each piece of this quilt is just like the provinces or states that separate us. Even though sometimes your tears make it seem like we're oceans and continents away. Maybe even galaxies. So take this carefully woven swatch of fabric and think of me whenever it's in your grasp. Wrap your body in it, until the day that I can do that.

"Were you ever in love with me?"

He chuckled faintly. "Yes... so bad it hurt. It still does sometimes."

"Why are you laughing?" She said as though his laughter were cruel.

"It will always be funny to me."

She looked at him blankly. He stepped closer and gently pulled her hand to his lips, looking into her eyes as they welled up with water. She was never good at holding back her tears. They always came without warning.

"It's funny because we loved each other so much we couldn't stand it, so we left. We went our separate ways, fucked other people, thought we'd fallen in love with so many others, just to see each other again and realize — we never moved on. We loved each other so insanely that it made us depart. I think that's funny."

And of course, he didn't really find that funny. It was more one of those things that you can only laugh at because it happened a long time ago and things are better now, at least. In reality the bittersweet moment both had them resenting the time they had not been able to spend together. It didn't seem fair that they lost years looking for the right taste between the wrong thighs and the right lap with the wrong guys. It didn't seem fair that they lost seconds, minutes, hours without each other because life is already so short, and their habits are already so life threatening. They might only have today.

There are a lot of different ways that I'd like to tell you I love you, I need you, I want you, you're everything, you're all that's important to me, you're all my life requires and you're all I could have hoped for, but all that ever comes out is: *Stay.*

WHEN YOU'RE NEAR AND
WHEN YOU'RE NOT

Hours should feel longer,
each minute I should ache
I should think in-between seconds,
with the image of your face
The eagerness of wanting to be with you,
should erupt within me— I should quake,
with a plethora of vibrations
from my head to down each leg
my hollow chest should echo
the words I love to hear you say
'I miss you,
          when you are away'
I should miss you
how the word 'miss' doesn't explain

          and sometimes,
          I do and I don't.

MY HAND

They sat quietly in the car in only the sound of the stereo and a brush of air through the slightly cracked back window on the lefthand side. She dazed off as she stared into the abyss, her eyes on the passing trees and occasional road signs but her vision somewhere deep in the back of her mind.

Her thoughts broke as she felt something shuffle her hand. She looked down and his fingers gently slid in between hers and with no words they shared a moment. She subtly sucked in her bottom lip as she tried not to smile.

The rest of the car ride was uneventful, but she spent the remainder of the night thinking about him and her hand in his.

"I THOUGHT YOU WOULDN'T LIKE ME BECAUSE OF MY WEIGHT"

She shied away.

"I don't care about your weight! Are you happy?" He pushed.

"Yeah.."

"Then so am I. I want to love you as long as you love you"

She couldn't explain why this sent chills up her spine. She looked at his slender figure and model-Esq features. He was nearly flawless. For the longest time she wondered, how could he want to be with her out of all the women he had to choose from. Why would he choose fat, over beautiful. She thought deeply. Because, *'I'm both.'*

I GUESS I JUST WANT TO BE LOVED

I don't want to fight, I don't want to have to stress, I don't want to think. I want the love between us to come naturally. I want to be stronger than ever through the toughest times and feel like they truly are my other half. I want them to know me better than I know myself.

I hate surprises but for the life of me I wish someone would surprise me with an act of love that is better than I could have ever imagined. I want to be loved in the way that would comfort me in my loneliness in the absence of them. I want to be loved in the way they are my muse and I am theirs.

I want to be loved in the way that my eyes see no one else but them, and their eyes, just me. I want to hold hands, lie in silence, go on dates just because, serenade one another, and smile because you're with them and how could that not make you smile.

I guess I just want to be loved, properly.

WEAK DAYS

Your ghost still lives here, even though you've been gone a long time, your ghost still makes the same conscious steps that you did, pacing back and forth but aware of where the floor would creak. First step, nothing, second step, nothing, third step, nothing, but every forth step you'd be so deep in thought you stepped on the loudest part of the floor. I'd hear it from downstairs, drinking my midnight coffee through a straw, because you were irritated enough with my caffeine habit, you didn't want it staining my teeth too. I still drink through a straw even though you're not here to hound me. It started to taste better this way. The springs on your bed still stretch and contract, on their own, at 1:16am when you went to sleep and 11:04 when you'd wake up. Except on saturdays, on saturdays your ghosts warmth covers me the way your stretched arm did across my body, the way your relaxed breath did on the back of my neck. I stay in bed longer now, waiting for your ghosts stomach to growl, waiting for you to get up before me this time, because now that it's your ghost I'm afraid if I leave it'll get the hint that you never did. Thinking about it now, maybe you did get the hint, that I tried to rush out of bed with you, so it didn't *seem* like that was where I wanted to be; even though it was. Perhaps you knew I rushed down to the kitchen on saturday mornings before your stomach could growl so I could make breakfast and you might believe I always knew what you were thinking. Maybe you knew that I wanted you to smell the food, come downstairs, sit across from me and look at me with those big brown eyes. Perhaps those mornings you saw my desperation, the desire I had to be more than we were, that maybe our saturday could be every day of the week. But even your ghost and I are foreign then.

39

I, YOU

I think you will say it, until I feel it. I think you will whisper it, scream it, sing it until it is the melody that plays a never-ending round in my head. I think you will say it, until I am guilted. I think you will say it, until I am quilted into your carefully woven words. I think you will fuck it into my mind until I've come to the conclusion that, I feel it too. I think you will say it until – it is me. Until those words, are me. Until those words replace my words. I think you will say it, until I am brain washed, but not clean to the dirty thoughts you put with mine. I think you will say I love you, until it kills me.

THE SLIGHTEST TOUCH

In that first instance touching your skin —
it made me question every other thing I had ever
come into contact with, that at the time,
I thought was perfect
It made every feeling before you vanish.
I didn't remember anything, not my joys, not my harms
                    and this was just from grazing arms.

"Would you go out with me?"

He asked sweetly.

"No thank you" She responded as she spun her tea bag in her cup by the string.

"No thank you?"

"Relationships are much too much thinking. What's wrong with us drinking tea together as two single people? We have fun don't we?"

"Yes.. But that's why I wan–"

"Do you actually want to date me?" She raised her brow, "Think about it. On christmas and birthdays you have the obligation of getting me a gift. You have to talk to me everyday even if you feel like curling up in bed and shutting out the world. If you take me out to dinner, you'll open doors, pay for my food and pretty much empty your wallet whenever we want to have fun. You'll be forced to hold my hand, give me kisses and do all the things I want just so you can please me."

"I would do those things with pleasure."

She looked at him impressed and half smiling. She leaned slightly over the counter and he obliged. They kissed softly and he smiled in between them.

"You're a foolish boy." She smiled, "But, we'll make this mistake together"

I love you, though

"I WOULD DIE FOR YOU"

He ensured her.

"I know. That's the problem." She said

"What is?"

"The fact that you would die for me.. the fact you would put your life on the line for me. It's absolutely stupid."

"That's not the reaction I was expecting..."

"I wouldn't know.. but.. dying seems easy. It just.. ends. No sadness, or pain after you're gone.. you're gone.. you're.. sleeping, just forever. But when you lose someone, you live in pain.. you grieve, you mourn, sometimes you never get over it.

So when you say that is something you would happily do for me, pardon me for not being as enthused as you had hoped. I love you and I will not allow you to put my life above yours. And if you try to pull something like that again... I will kill you."

He cracked a smile before fading into a serious expression.

"Why do you get to put your life on the line for everyone else, then? How is that fair?"

"It's not. Not really. It's all selfish in the long run... I want to be a hero, and if I live to be a hero again.. even better."

PERSPECTIVE

"You know me so well" They stared at each other fighting back a grin, "It scares the shit out of me. I don't know when I became an open book but—"

"You are *not* an open book." He interrupted, "I spent weeks just trying to get you to talk to me about something that mattered to you. I couldn't figure out why you weren't as simple as the people you surrounded yourself with. I couldn't understand any of it. If anyones an open book. I am. I fell for you trying to make you fall for me."

She froze in a moment of euphoria. Her tongue couldn't taste the butterflies that fluttered deep inside of her. She couldn't comprehend how she felt, she couldn't explain how she kept falling for him with never having fallen out. All she knew, was him.

"Why did you want me to fall for you?"

"I've never had someone see beneath my surface the way you did."

BATTLE

It's terrible to love you. It's terrible to love you when you are loved by so many others. It's terrible because I don't want to share you. I don't want to have to fight for you just to notice me, and then fight to find something in myself that is worth you loving. It's terrible. But I realized after all of this and after everything I've been through with or without you, but since you – I've found myself. I know who I am when I'm with you is who I want to be all the time. You made me a fighter. You made me a survivor. You made me the person who doesn't give up no matter how bad it gets and no matter how badly I want to. The key to my successes are always you. You are forever changing and challenging me and I'm always growing. You are unconquerable and so I always have something to work towards. You are the prize of the battle I never get tired fighting for.

MARRY ME

When you're ready. Watch me walk down the aisle happier than I've ever been. Hold my shaking hands as I hold back my tears of joy. Recite to me on our big day how you can't wait to start our future. How you didn't think we would make it this far but you're glad we did. How you are more surprised than anyone that it was us that ended up together. Then, I'll tell you that I always knew. I'll tell you that I had no doubts that you were the only one I could ever wake up to, and so before I had you – I chose to wake up alone. I'll tell you in front of everyone that I've loved you since I was 15. I'll tell you that sometime between then and now I figured out: you weren't my first but you would be my last. I'd tell you, that's all I ever needed was for you to be who I ended up with. You were the only. You are the only one. So when you're ready to marry me – you don't even have to ask.

When I Run Out of Things to Write About

When I run out of things to write about in the dead of the night, I look over as you sleep next to me. I get struck with inspiration. The way your eyebrows dagger above your closed eyes. The ones that; while open, are evergreen on sage on a honey golden brown. The ones like sinking sand; I get trapped in them. I look at the hundreds of lashes that fall on the subtle bags of your eyes, but also your cheeks that force your eyes shut when you smile. I focus on the dimple, but not-really-dimple near the crevice of your faint rose-colored lips. I've noticed how even when your mouth is pressed together you can still see the corners of your teeth, almost like you're smiling at me. When I think I've run out of things to write about, I remember everything in the sight of you. I get lost in every burnt umber strand of your hair, and I leave thoughts in there for the next time I need inspiration. I try to do you justice but; you are far more beautiful than the art I create.

NARROW

I've always wondered
out of all the people you meet,
how do you narrow it down
to just one to be with?
And then I found
them.
And from then on,
I stopped wondering that, and
now I wondered:
out of all the people you meet –
what made you narrow it down to me?

I CAN'T LIE

I want you in my bed,
resting your head
where I dream of us
maybe my pillow
will be a muse
that encourages you
to do it too

Like once,
I dreamed that
our lips met
before we did

I dreamed that
our hearts
were conjoined
before we linked hands
that one time,
we parted through a crowd.

I mean, I know
that wasn't an advance,
but that night I went home, and

I dreamed that,
you might be in my bed
using my pillow as a muse
and completing your dues
of maybe, loving me too.

CURVES

Your hands slid
along each dip of my skin
you gripped
on my hips
and I raised up
my chin
and we were,
lips to lips,
skin to skin,
pulse's synchronized,
and we
were falling in
to each others sin —

And we basked
in the rise
of my curves.

ADMIRE

I just want to admire you
I want to stare at you
while you lie next to me.

I want to wonder
what amazing images
your dreams withhold.

I want you to be,
the only thing that
makes sense —

When my world,
is upside down
You are right side up.

I don't need to
kiss you, to feel
my tulips bloom

I just want to admire you
as long as I'm breathing
while you lie next to me.

Can I kiss your wounds;
succumb the infection,
reverse the damage
and sew you back together
good as new.
Like you never knew,
or'd even know
you were broken once?

"Tall chai tea latte and a bagel - cream cheese?"

We both reached for it and awkwardly looked at one another. I glanced up at him and wondered if I had heard the order wrong, but there it was. My exact order in the hands of the café girl.

"Um.. for Thomas?" She finished.

Slightly embarrassed I let him grab it. He looked down at it for a moment and then held it out to me with a smile.

"Go ahead, have it. I'll wait for yours"

"Thanks" I said still red in the face, "See ya.."

I walked far into the corner of the café and sat down as I hid behind my book. About ten minutes had passed and I noticed him still waiting for my order. Meanwhile, I was halfway through my tea and my bagel was nearly done. Or, should I say his bagel.

"Uh.. Riley?" I peered over my book, "It's written on the cup. I didn't stalk you or anything."

"Oh, sorry it took so long for you to get.."

"No worries, but do you think I could sit with you? Over the wait it seemed to get pretty crowded."

Now I'm really not the type to talk to strangers but I did feel as though I owed him. He waited fifteen minutes for a bagel. As he looked at me with his big hazel eyes I gestured for him to sit. He pulled out the chair and took his bag off and shoved it under the table. He immediately dug into his food and scarfed it down as though he hadn't eaten in days. I felt even worse suddenly.

"I just want to say thank you.." I said quietly, "For giving me your order."

"Oh don't even worry about it. It seems like you enjoyed it, so it was worth it." He said nonchalantly before taking another large bite, "So Riley, that's an interesting name for a girl."

"It is?"

"I don't know, maybe"

I looked up at him as I saw him searching for the right words. His thick but clean kept eyebrows moved theatrically as he appeared to be deep in thought. I tried to stare longer as I slightly shielded my glance with my book. I saw him nearing the end of his food and I felt myself for a moment, miss his company already. I didn't want him to leave.

He crumpled up his wrapper as he chewed, took a sip of his tea and swallowed the remains. He began to stand up and he threw his bag over his shoulder.

"Well, I'm heading out. It was nice to meet you."

"It was nice to meet you too.." I said with disappointment in my voice, "See ya.."

He waved and walked out. I put my book down as I could no longer focus on these words when so many others were filling my mind. As I rested it down I noticed his cup holder there, he had written on it:

Maybe you can take my dinner sometime.

555-8629

-Thomas

"All I know is if you want this to work, it can." He said as the cold air began to nip at our ears, "I don't care what anyone else thinks."

I felt it right then. Normally at this point I would dig in the dark corners of my mind for all the noncommittal responses I could think of. But in the moment I was most certain that, he was what I wanted. His words turned to warmth as we sat closely together on the park bench.

"I don't care either."

FOREIGN

He stared at her intently as he listened to her speak.

"You sound so different. It's like your foreign."

She smiled as she picked at a loose thread on her sock, "You've always been foreign to me."

"How?"

"You use to love me and that was most mysterious of all. I just wish that when you did, I had taken the time to appreciate it." Her eyes crept up as she glanced at him, "Instead of run from it."

READ ME

I want to be a book that gets read cover to cover. I want to be a book that's words linger in your mind always. I want to be a book that changes your outlook on – everything. I want to be your prized possession that you keep in a showcase or on the top shelf away from idle hands. I want to be a book that you read again and again – and again; because understanding me will continue to be fascinating. I want you to love my story, and caress my thoughts as they coddle the pages. I want to be in your hands as you skim over my pages like my flesh is written in braille. Read me.

It's the thought that counts

I do not know enough words
to tell you all the things I feel for you

I do not have enough days left
to say them, if I did

I do not encompass the courage
I'd need to say them

and so,
I do not have a clue –
why the things I'd say would matter to you.

WITH ME

You feel like my favorite song sounds,
you're the only thing that makes my day function
and the only tune that goes 'round in my mind

You taste how my favorite pillow feels,
you're the only thing that can make me dream
and the only time I sleep without fear

You look how sunday morning brunch smells
You smell how the sun and a light breeze feels
I know a lot of this is confusing; I'm trying to say I guess —

You just fit alright with me.

THE DISTANCE NEVER MATTERED

You loved me once;
do you remember that?
Cyber kisses, wishes
and online naps

The distant times
we lived in different days
watching the same sun
when it came my way

The late night chats
and how we longed;
the naive beliefs;
If you were here –
If I was there;
we could do no wrong

The wanting stares
at our laptop screen
dying to be held –
wanting to scream

You loved me once,
I remember that
and it's time you knew
I loved you back.

I CANYON'T LIE

I have a crush on you,
the kind of crush that would
cause my bones to crumble into dust,
from a 6 thousand foot drop

The kind of crush that would
make me chase you 277miles – on foot,
just to breathe the same air as you.

I have a crush on you,
the size of the grand canyon
and despite it being one of the
Seven Natural Wonders of the World,
you're the only one
I'd jump for

and you make me wonder more.

I WANNA KNOW WHEN YOU FELL

When you first looked at them
and the thought "damn, I love you"
was hemmed into your head

Was it when,
they read
and put their nerdy glasses on
Was it the way
they sang the wrong lyrics,
to their 'favorite' song

Was it when,
they drank their tea
and burned their tongue
because they thought
they'd grow old waiting,
and wanted to die young

Was it the way
they gazed at their reflection,
like they're trying to understand
who they are,
and why the line of their love has never
stretched quite long enough on their hands?

Or maybe it was when,
you were loving who you were
when they would hold you
and this feeling, this love,
this whole world with them
wouldn't exist, with the old you

Under you

I'm gonna get over you,
but do you remember
when I was under?

When I was weighed
beneath,
your skin
when I leaned up
into your kisses,

When your love
spilled over me
like it was
the running current
of a river that never slowed
and always ran, as though
it were afraid it's true
thoughts might catch up with it.

It washed out my sadness
with every wave.
It was beautiful.
Though, I'll get over you.
But don't forget – when I was under.

His hands
Gripped my waist like a belt,
Except I came undone

My lips have not kissed,
nor uttered quite enough words
to show you how much more
I deserve you, than her.

ADORN

I want someone
to fall completely
and utterly
in love,
with what a mess
I am.

I want them,
to stupidly grin,
when I'm silly.

to blush,
when I'm sweet.

but mostly,
just to be in love..
with me.

I think,
some part of me,
somewhere deep down
needs you
to be imperfect.
So I have a reason
not to love you,

But I guess the truth is, to me
you *are* perfect, and **I do**.

AWAITED

One day, you will look at them
in a way you never have before; not once.
You will see things in them so remarkable,
shock will smother you, as you ask yourself
how on earth you ever missed such a thing.

Life will dawn on you,
their existence — once a shadow —
will become that which casts it.
Your chest will thud as if someone on the inside
is banging, barging, brawling to get out;
and they will.

When they do, you will feel every ounce
of love that was bled, dripped and seeped for you
that you refused to douse yourself in.
It will hit you like a ton of bricks,
and one by one as you free yourself
from the ignorance you've lived and breathed so long,

you will see, the one who's always
awaited you, has been
right under your nose
            — since day one

COMPASSION

I didn't think I needed you,
I thought I could do it on my own.
but the weight of the world is twice as much
when you carry it alone.

I thought that you were an addition,
not my other half..
but we were a package deal,
the compass and the map.

See now I don't know where I'm going,
I don't know which way I'm due.
my path changes almost always,
I think my compass is showing me you.

RAINY STAYS

It is the rain
that drips your name
but can't wash away
the taint
or impressions you've made
          on my skin.

It can hush my cries
by blending in
and it makes me
want to fall in —
          love with you.

Under the night sky
that's the darkest blue,
with rain appearing out of nowhere,
just like you..
               did

You consume me,
outside and in
I can't fathom,
how amazing that's been
          to know

The rain drips your name
and like you, it comes
and goes by surprise –
but stays for a show

FALLIN' OUT

Am I, as easy to fall in
as I am, to fall out of love with?
Will my bed be as easy to sneak out of,
as it was to be guided in?
Is my heart as replaceable,
as the one you switched with mine?
Will I be back to the person,
who you just asked for the time?
Will you fall out as quickly,
as you found yourself falling in?
Will I be as disposable as,
in the past I had been?

ON SCREEN

I want to love in scenes,
how love looks on screen
I want to be as tense as the glances
and the air in between,
I want to be the heavy breathing,
when all thoughts can be seen

I want to be the nights with a stranger
that feel like endless love,
the mind-numbing, throat tightening,
fear stricken, most worthwhile thing
you could think of

I want my life to have a soundtrack
for each emotion, each dream,
each time consuming thought,
and my final epiphany
I want to love in scenes,
how love looks on screen.

I haven't forgotten you, not yet

not ever,
If I'm being honest
I don't and wont
forget the things you said
or what they meant
and that they meant
something to me
and to *you*, enough
for you to say them
because
if I'm being honest
not ever,

Not yet, have I forgotten you.

I'LL LOVE YOU IF YOU WANT ME TO

I'll love you if you want me to
I'll give you everything I have,
a few items in my pocket,
some jokes that'll make you laugh

I can cook and bake up a storm
I can also feed you in other ways,
I'm not bad at writing poetry
and I'll cater to you on your birthdays

I'll put in all my effort,
I promise I'll do my very best..
I'll love you wholeheartedly,
but you should probably know the rest:

I'll love you like I promised
but somedays it wont seem so,
my arms used to hug you,
will push you as far as you can go.

My lips once used to kiss you,
will utter things obscene
my love for myself will not exist
so it'll make me really mean.

So I'll love you, if you want me to..
It'll hurt good, a lot, and true
but if you really want my love,
I'll give it all to you.

I saw the moon move yesterday
when I looked up to the night sky
and it lit up the entire town
my mum said it was the clouds
and that the moon doesn't move
at that speed right before our eyes

and it made me want to cry
to deny that she was right
because it reminded me of me –
life passing me by,
and feeling like I'm standing, still
not with you.

DON'T LET ME MAKE
THE SAME MISTAKES AGAIN

There is a boy who loves me, he tells me everyday
stubborn as I am, I tell him it's his mistake
But nothing will convince him; none of my flaws
none of the wounds on the days I have claws
He loves my imperfections and explores all my parts
curiously admiring me like a piece of modern art

Unconditionally loved; like I could do no wrong
expecting of me, only that I am never gone
He treasures the things, I thought were a bore
though when I'm not trying at all, it's what he adores
When he pours his heart out there's a lump in my throat
sometimes I drown in his emotions and sometimes I float

He loves me, and I love that it's true
but embracing love is hard, when a battle fights in you.

You make me write

You make me write the kind of words that I can barely choke out, the kind of words that collect tears in my eyes but force me to blindly write through them. You make me write the kind of words I'll look back on months from then and remember how strongly I felt and realize I have never loved you more than I do today. You make me write the kind of words that are honest, and show my most hidden self. You open me up; I become an open book and you're always the only one brave enough to look. You make me write words that change others the way you've changed me. You make me write words that bring me clarity. You are these words, you make me write – you. And I have, in a thousand different ways, for each day you served a different purpose. Discovering my passion, my heart, my calling and myself. You make me write.. I don't think you know what that means.

I'M NOT:

That ditzy, lovey, clingy,
hung up, love sick, love struck girl
when I'm in love

I'm that terrified, Alice in wonderland
drug trip – crazy *and* my reality is different from yours

And for me to have fallen down the rabbit hole
would mean that I stopped paying attention
to maintaining the brick of the wall that separates me
from the people who could hurt me

It means missing you, wanting you,
loving everything about you, can't eat, can't sleep –
is my punishment

and the only way I'll win is if you can love me
regardless of my attitude; my apathetic tendencies,
my need to be alone, my swings of moods,
and the fact I don't want to need you

But no one ever can, so, I'm just not the girl
with anything to show for it, in the end.

FOREVER IS A SEVEN LETTER WORD

Forever is how long I thought that I was doing people a favor by telling them I was broken before they pursued me. Thinking I was saving them from getting hurt trying to pick up the pieces. But I think, I think that I was never broken, just slightly cracked and I thought I was too delicate to be touched.

Originally I thought that the imperfections of me made me not worth it.. but all it meant is that life threw me around a bit and I was getting handed a break.

Reasons for bad things don't always seem clear, but the good things, you just shouldn't question.

Everyone, no matter how badly they've been hurt, or no matter if they've hurt someone else, deserves to be loved, by whomever chooses to love them.

Vacant souls seem to be everywhere.. ones dying to hold someone close to them. And I didn't know that I was one of them until I finally felt myself caring about someone more than myself.

Every day my thoughts were devoted to them and I wanted to be my best. I wanted to be all they thought I was to begin with:

Real. Just someone who understood that we can't choose who we love, but we can choose what we do about it.

LONGING

Do you know how much I love you, hurts? Did you know sometimes I crave to have your hand holding mine. I want to be in your arms and I want you to protect me from this world because you use to once. You use to be all I ever needed to protect me from everyone else, and mostly from myself. But you became the villain and I still love you. You're bad. And I still love you. You're wrong for me. And I still love you. It's over. I'm not coming back and neither are you. I still love you. You ruined me, but I still love you.

SAY ANYTHING

I just needed you to open your mouth, to somehow show that you need me. I needed you to tell me anything that told me not to walk away. But in everything you didn't say and in everything you didn't do, I felt you letting me float away. And today, I wished you would have said anything.

I don't want to be liked.
I want to be loved.
And I want *you* to be the one who loves me.

MATTER

I guess it just seems,
as though I don't matter,
not because it's true,
nor because of you..

but rather:

because you never call
never write,
hardly laugh,
you're nowhere in sight
and you hardly talk to me..

so I guess it just seems,
as though I don't matter
not because it's true,
nor because of you..

but rather:

because you're gone
and I've gone so long
pretending
this is a love worth
defending

so I guess it just seems,
as though *it* don't matter,
not because it's true,
nor because of you..

but rather:

because I die,
every time I cry
and I'm not going to lie,
and say that it don't matter.

IF SHE WALKS AWAY

Don't think it's because she wants to
don't assume she is done with you
she is likely muttering to herself
"Please, stop me"

All you have to do is say something:
'Oh so you're just going to walk away from this?'
'Wait!'
'Wait, I love you'
'Coward'
Anything you say,
good or bad, will let you keep her;
I promise you.

Just don't let her think,
you'd rather let her disappear forever,
than to fight with her sometimes
because that's not true is it?

You actually kinda like when she yells,
and it turns into a cry..
and her nose gets red,
you want to kiss her in that moment
you can't believe she's so passionate with you
when she writes other peoples bullshit off.

She puts in the effort with you
so if she walks away
say something
she'll have to stay
because you know
and she knows,
she never really wanted to walk away.

I love you too much,
too immensely,
too willfully,
too recklessly,

I love you to –
death.

WET NOSES AND WINDOW SILLS

The days it rains
and the house is cold
it reminds me of
you holding me
when I cried into you

I couldn't keep all my troubles
to myself anymore
I was weak
but strong enough to trust you

So everyday it rains
it reminds me of how I drained
all my problems
into the fabrics of your shirt
as I rubbed my runny nose
you only looked down at me
as if you were
wishing you could do more

and each day it rains
I wished you were here
for me to tell you it was enough

A LOT, SO MUCH & MORE

I can't take the way I feel when revelations of love are admitted. Whether they are for me, or for someone else. In many ways I am just ungrateful, or unprepared for the journey of requited love. Must I be unselfish and give myself to them? When they give themselves to me, what do I do with them?

Do I feed them? Walk them? What do they need? I'm not ready to worry about someone more than just me. I can't breathe with that kind of responsibility. I don't know what to do while my space is invaded, I didn't think this was normal. I didn't know my lips could belong to someone on the morning of lazy sundays. I didn't know my chest would be bombarded with kisses I didn't condone.

I didn't know. I didn't know my ears would hear the sound of someones bated breaths and shuffles in my bed that normally only accommodated my curves in the mattress. Though, now a new body is contorting the springs.

I'm not good at hearing confessions of undying love. Though they're beautiful. When admitted to the girl a table away from me, I feel bad for myself. For never having someone love me like that. When admitted to me, I feel scared for myself. For never having someone tell me, *just because that one time in high school that guy pretended to love you just to get in your pants,* doesn't mean this guy, right here in front of you – confessing his love, is like that.

I'm silly and not worth it, but then I know that's not true. But no matter how positive I try to be, it's all my mind is running through. And so I'm worthless and silly, I don't deserve to be yours. Because while I give you nothing, you would give me purpose; a lot, so much and more.

I just fear that
a year from now
you'll have lived the tales
of many men
and I'll have lived none,
dreaming of only one —

you.

DAD

The way he looked at me in disgusted disapproval. He will never be proud of me. I sometimes wonder what would happen if I actually did something bad rather than just not doing something well enough. Would I be shunned completely? I don't get the reason everyone sees my intelligence except him. I have tried so hard to put myself out there, to show him I am able, to show him I was raised well, in great parts to my mother. Though, in search of a desperate need for mutual love; thanks to him too.

His tough conditional love paved an eggshell path. I've bled countless unrealistic talents that didn't quite fit me right, just to be someone he would claim. I've swallowed my tears when the grades I slaved to earn weren't enough. I plastered on a smile that still shames me to this day because he cares too much for people to know he has unhappy kin. But cares not enough about the reason behind the unhappiness.

Many have told me to live for myself, because to live life for the approval of someone else will be the death of me. They are right, because I am dying. We all are, but my energy, my liveliness, my hope and aspirations, my dreams – they are all withering away. Where has my passion gone. And when will I be enough, Dad?

I MISS YOU MORE

I miss you more
than the moon misses the stars in a city sky.
I miss you more
than I thought I would and more than you miss I.

I miss you like an emptiness
I thought I'd never feel.
I miss you so bad sometimes
I can't believe it's real.

I miss you more,
than the picnics, I know you use to take.
I miss you more,
than I imagined, I miss your fucking face.

I miss you.. like, it's crazy,
I'm appalled at just how bad.
I miss you and I want to cry,
and it's getting kind of sad.

Tu me manques: You are missing from me

You are missing from me –
whoever you are

The other heart
that is the puzzle piece,
that connects to mine.
I miss you,
though I'm not sure
you know me yet.
You make me smile,
and laugh, a lot.
You hold me,
even though I act unaffectionate
because you know,
my distance is just a cry,
for help,
for love,
for compassion,
but all of those things,

seem to be missing from me
and so are you.

Memories of you taste like broken glass

WHEN WE WERE DIFFERENT PEOPLE

I wonder what you're like now,
I wonder if you still wish at 11:11
with the silly hope all your dreams will come true,
and then patiently waiting as that reality dances
in your thoughts, to the music
with each wavering chord you drown your mind in.
You always find a way to simmer in the precious silence
after the song in your head crescendos,
with the genuine belief, your dreams are on their way;
I admire that.
So, I wonder if you're like that still,
if that shooting star that I wished you saw too,
came into your line of view.
Maybe you wished I saw it too, if you —
still think of me that is.
I wore out the threads of your existence,
you're everything I wish I could be,
so every blown out candle,
every penny in a wishing well,
every shooting star, every 11:11;
I wish you're wishing for me

EVENTUALLY

It'll stop hurting,
secrets will be safe,
hearts will mend,
tears will dry,
life will organize,
suns will rise,
wings will fly,
simplicity will commence
mouths will smile
dreams will flourish
hope will find you —
eventually.

I WONDER

I think about what you're thinking about,
even after you leave.
I wonder if you're thinking about
how much you think about me.

I wonder if how I ignored you,
made you feel weak.
I wonder if you felt incomplete
at how well I seemed to be –

      without you.

I wonder if you're hurt.
If I could repair you at the seam.
I care, about where,
you end up, you see.

I wonder if you think that,
now I feel free.
That staying with you,
would have been the death of me.

But I wonder
if you wondered anything
about me,
      mostly.

NOT ALIVE

I forget sometimes, that I'm alive
as I sit in my own skin,
I see my hands, my fingers type
out of body; headphones in.

I'm in all these conversations,
my brain manages to respond.
On autopilot for the last 8 months,
my mind is almost gone.

I don't remember, really,
why or when things changed.
But when I look at old photos
I wished we were the same.

ONE BY ONE

My world was a night sky
    absent of anything
    that would lead you to believe
    your eyes were even open

and one day, one by one;
    your lips that curved into a smile
    put stars into my sky
    and a little light into my eyes

but as time went on
    the nights got brighter, I doubted
    the appeal that'd be revealed in my presence
    I had grown comfortable hidden in the dark

and so one day, one by one;
    I put out the stars between my finger tips
    they dissolved like snowflakes on warm tongues
    and I slipped back into the absent night sky

    I think about you sometimes,
    but even if I chose to let the light back in to someone new
        I would never see another quite like you

I'm not lonely because you're there;
I'm lonely because
When you cry, when you hurt, when you laugh,

when you breathe —

I am here.

I'M IN LOVE WITH THE IDEA

I'm in love with the idea
of being with someone who can make me laugh.
I'm in love with the idea
of being with someone who can
call me in the morning to chill
do nothing and have fun still.
I'm in love with the idea
of having someone who won't hurt me
the way the rest have.

But I was just in love with an idea
that wasn't in love with me

WALTZ

"Will you dance with me?"

I looked up to his welcoming palm and I took it gracefully. As we walked to the dance floor I noticed most of the room watching us. The entire night I felt everyone invited to the wedding was wondering when we would finally dance. His hands were clammy but I didn't mind. As my fingers lapped over his shoulders he stared into my eyes before resting his forehead against mine. Our batting lashes brushed briskly against each other and we both smiled as I shied away. The hand he had rested on my waist pulled my hips to his and I downed the lump in my throat. He tilted my head up with his and he flicked the bottom of my top teeth with his tongue. My mouth curled into a smile. His hand sheltered my left cheek as his thumb scaled my jaw and his other hand soon mirrored that as he pulled me in for a kiss. My feet stopped in place and others continued to dance around us as I felt my whole world stand still. I had never truly deeply closed my eyes during a kiss until this very moment, and his lips tasted like forever. Whatever that means. But I could feel forever in his lips.

WHOLE

In almost every aspect of the word, I am whole.
I have ten fingers, ten toes, both eyes, ears, a nose
and quite a mouth on me, my mother says.
But I'm not whole in ways of fulfillment
in which these blessings should offer me, or rather
in which ways I should utilize them
I'm not whole in the way that allows me
to use my heart to love another full time.
I cannot even love myself for half of that, and to me
someone with ten fingers to touch hearts,
ten toes to run to opportunities,
both eyes, ears and a nose to experience life
through all it's vices and virtues
should be more than capable of loving another
of the worlds greatest gifts – a human soul

But I can't always, I don't always
I won't sometimes ..

I think because the thing about being whole is,
there's always a hole. A part of me in which
has not graced my presence yet, a piece that is missing
I need it to be who I'm suppose to be,
the appendages, organs, annoying habits; the works
I need to know this part of me, to know if
I'd be the sort of person who jumps in front of a bullet
for a friend, or if I hide and drop behind a chair
I want to know if I am brave, if I am capable
If I'm truly a poet who has a story to share
If I will survive depression on the worst nights
If I will pick and choose my fights, but never raise a fist
or my voice but rather improve my argument
I want to know what my darkness is in the light, and
If I am who I've always wished I could be —
Whole; in every aspect of the word.

LOOK FOR ME

I wish someone wanted to find me,
I wish that while I was chasing the one I loved,
they were chasing me.

I want to realize in my many attempts
to be that persons one and only,
that someone was trying to be mine.

I would hope that the one I was chasing
eventually showed me they are unworthy of my love,
and I would realize there is someone who is..

and they had been looking for me –
     all along.

SOMETIMES

Sometimes it feels better,
    sometimes it's just okay,
    sometimes I wanna end it all
    on the days I fade away

Sometimes I forget
    there's nothing I can do,
    sometimes I just embrace
    all I am because of you

Sometimes it's like it's over,
    and I should just give up.
    Sometimes I ignore that voice
    yours is the only one I trust

Sometimes, more than often,
    if not everyday I breathe,
    I just wonder if you're still in love,
    or maybe it's just me.

OKAY-SIONALLY

Occasionally,
    I think about you,
    I wish that I had held on
             tighter
    That I had been a fighter,
    when it came to us,
    but I wasn't, because I
    trusted
    no one, and
    the trials thrust upon me,
    made me lose faith
    in the entire human race.
    So, okay..
    I think about you,
    but only because,
    so much of my youth was spent,
    fawning over you,
    but, I don't do that anymore.
    I don't believe in that,
             Okay?
    Occasionally I think I still do,
    but how can I believe in love,
    when all I've ever wanted,
    and the only one I've ever loved
    didn't want me enough
    to stay when I was so scared
    I pushed you away.
    You should have known!
    You should have known,
    all I wanted was for you
    to tell me to stay,
    to tell me you loved me too,
             occasionally.

MADNESS;

the war in which,
who shall battle and win,
the madness in love
or the body it lives in?

I don't think with my heart.
Love passes me by sometimes.

AT THE SAME TIME

Why do I love you and
hate you at the same time?
Why do I want you to roam free
but wish you were still mine?
Why can't I forget you
and how you were so fine?
Why does hate and love
seem to be such a fine line?

I HATE SO MUCH ABOUT YOU

I hate so much about you
everyday you make me mad
and the days I'm free from anger
are the ones you've made me sad.

I hate how you don't get me
and how you laugh when I'm in pain
I don't like the way you talk to me
or the way you say my name.

I don't like when you make promises
I know you'll never keep
I wish you'd just shut up sometimes
for longer than a sleep.

I hate that you're tied to me
that you think I was a gift
I hate that you think the fact I've stayed
is a sign we shouldn't quit.

I hate the way you talk sometimes
when you think you know it all
I hate when I'm on your pedestal
and I love it when I fall

I love when you admit I'm not perfect
so I hate you most of the time
I hate when you believe me
the times I say I'm fine

God, I hate so much that you do
and when you hold me to the ground
But the one thing I hate more than that, oddly —
is when you're not around

Paper mache

Why do we keep trying, when we
fight
When we,
cry
When we,
forget that hearts aren't made out of paper mache,
and they aren't meant to be wounded
because candy wont fall out,
but hope will,
love will,
life will.

Why do we keep trying, when we
fight
When we,
cry
When we,
forget that hearts aren't made out of paper mache;
we still think like little kids
and believe nothing can touch us.

But we fight,
we cry,
we forget,
that our hearts broke last time
and we wont survive it again.

IF YOU'VE EVER MISSED SOMEONE

and I'm certain you have;

You can probably relate to that sinking feeling in the pit of your stomach and the fact you just feel like an empty vessel with all this potential but nothing to occupy you.

You can probably relate to your denial, thinking that you're okay and filled with the silly belief that you've been coping rather well, not really acknowledging you've been avoiding things, people, pictures, places and songs that remind you of them. Because you know coming face to face with their existence is the one thing that will bring you crashing down.

If you've ever missed someone you can probably relate to the nostalgic nights and the sound of your own sobs as the world around you grows silent so that nothing is louder than your thoughts.

It finds a way to eat at you, devouring your flesh, and those times you try to pull it together before there's nothing left — sometimes it works.

Sometimes you just open your eyes to the next morning and deny they're gone all over again until the memory is too strong and you are too weak to deny that, you miss them —

you never stopped.

THREE WORDS I'LL NEVER LET YOU KNOW

I'm never going to love you,
or at least I'll never tell –
I can't fall for another
who claims to love me
but doesn't know me well

Don't count on me to say it
those words don't belong to me.
Nothing you'll do or say
nothing I'll feel for you,
will inhabit my vocabulary

You can treat me like a goddess
like I've only imagined in my dreams
but I will not succumb to my soul
and say those words –
you won't hear them from me

It may mean there is no future
no room for romance in my life
and you can say all you want –
however loud –
I will never be your wife

I've known since I was younger;
only take what you have earned
I won't close the gap, the distance,
utter the words; make me yours
Because it's not what I deserve.

113

MISSING YOU DOESN'T GO AWAY

It hurts worse than it did yesterday
more often than not.
Days that pass,
begin to feel like years,
that I can't grasp

Like as though,
they happened,
centuries ago

You're every memory
I cherish
each dream,
I pray'll come true
you're worth more
than I can fathom
you're what's old,
and what's new..

It's awful to miss you,
I fear it day and day
again and again..
but I know you deserve
a life away from me,
so I turn my back,
and count from ten..

10 - I adore you
9 - you make me laugh
8 - you're always kind
7 - you're all I have
6 - you always care
5 - you're all I need
4 - I keep wishing
3 - what you need is me,
2 - I don't want to turn around,
1 - I can't bare to watch you leave.

So when I get to zero,
Vanish, would you please?

Because missing you,
doesn't go away
but neither does the pain
of you regretting when you stay.

So, I guess that's it..
They're not you.

I fell for you, and
your love taught me gain.
I lost you, and
that loss caused me pain.

But I loved you, and
and that phase made me sane,
'Cause whether I laughed or I cried,
it all pleased me the same

I THINK I FALL IN LOVE
WITH EVERYONE I MEET

Even you, you, that guy I passed in the hall and thought it was nice that when you bumped into me, you smiled as you apologized. You, the one who bothered to learn my name when I was just your waitress. You, who helped me pick up my scattered papers as I chased them down on the train platform. You, who hugged me that one night when I was holding in my hurt. You, who paid for my drink. You, who said 'You're perfect'. You, who asked my dad for permission to ask me out on a date. You, for taking me on my first date. You, for defending me. You, for beating me, forcing me to be tougher and in result helping me win my first real fight. You, for saying you loved me even though you didn't mean it, but knowing I needed to hear it. You, for making me feel attractive and never keeping those words to yourself. You, for saying nothing to me in the awkward silences of our relationships, where I wished there was something to say because I wanted you so fucking bad. But, you were the one I loved that I didn't meet. But I fall in love with you, some how.. even the undesirable, the criminal, the evil... I love you all and it frightens me.

Do I miss being in love? I think it would be hard to miss something that happens so regularly, or at least is not in absence for too long. So, I guess what I miss is, being in love with someone who is in love with me.

I miss the mornings. Waking up with them on your mind and morning texts on your phone. I like the comfort you felt just knowing you had them at the end of the day. I miss how they were medicine to me. They fixed everything, even physical wounds I once inflicted on myself. Sometimes, without that love it's hard to find a distraction or a reason. I miss that they never forget to remind you, you matter. I miss being totally and utterly consumed with this persons image in my mind. I miss doing things for them, always and on special occasions. I miss missing them. I miss them being my muse. I miss feeling like finally my existence has a purpose and my love can go to someone who I feel truly deserves it. In those moments I have so much to give because of how much they give me. I love and require the reciprocation. I miss how fulfilling they make my life. I miss learning things together. I miss discovering with them. Life without love, even the love of a dream, is pointless.

So yes, I miss being in love, admittedly even with the ones who are not in love with me.

MISADVENTURE
&
MELANCHOLY

Happy?

Do you like it better when I'm real? When I admit how I feel? When I say no it's not okay you hang out with her, yes it makes me jealous. When I said have a good time I really meant I hope it's a miserable one. No I'm not happy. No I don't like doing that one thing you insist I do with you. No, you didn't treat me how I liked. Yes, I think about leaving you nearly every day. Why haven't I? Because I'm scared to hurt you. You're delicate and it scares me. I don't want you to kill yourself. But sometimes I think if it just happened, then I wouldn't worry so much. I think I would heal okay. Eventually. It would be easier than trying to give you something worth holding onto. Because it's not me. I'm worthless. I'm just a really really good actress, and I mimic what you really want. But to be honest I stay for your family, so they don't have to lose you. That and so I'm not responsible for a lost life. I don't want to give up on you, but for fuck sakes.. You just fuck up so much and it's so frustrating. I lie when I say nothing is wrong with you. There is plenty. But. You deserve someone who can love that about you. But it isn't me. So, now that you've heard my thoughts after my silence irritated you for so long.. do you feel better, or worse?

'TIL DEATH DO YOU PART

"– Together you guys can do anything. Congratulations you two. Cheers" I took a gulp of my wine as I barely made it through the toast with out revealing the shake in my voice.

I stepped off the stage and made it back to my table as the bride and the groom shared a dance. I accepted another refill of wine and made my way to the bathroom. The fluorescent lights hurt my eyes and I shut them off as I cried over the sink. I ran the water to drown the noise while I tried to collect myself.

"Amy?" The lights flicked on and the bride appeared at the door, "Hun, are you okay?"

"Hey.." I cleared my throat, "Yeah I'm great, I just got some makeup in my eye."

"Are you sure?" I nodded yes, "Well I just wanted to say thank you. Your toast meant so much, you're such a good friend to both of us. I'm glad we met"

"Me too" I smiled.

I couldn't hate her. She was so nice, so genuine. She really loved him, but so did I. But, I couldn't hate her. Regardless of the fact she had the only thing I ever wanted.

After she left I wiped my eyeliner from below my eyes and powdered my now red nose. I realized how old it was getting to cover up. Why was I still doing this to myself? I walked out of the bathroom with a new smile and new attitude thanks to my newly empty glass of wine.

"Aim, Amy?" I turned to see him; the groom. "Thank you."

"For what?"

"The toast. It meant so much and what you said was really beautiful"

"And you're surprised?" I raised my brow, "Because I'm the bitter ex, right?"

"Well, I know you like me so—"

"Exactly, I was kind *because* I like you" We stood in an awkward moment, "Look, I want you to be happy and if it's not me who makes you happy then, I shouldn't get to be with you."

He was silent and reluctantly looked me in the eyes. He looked like he had something to say but we both knew it wouldn't change anything.

HOW TO LOSE THE BITTERNESS OVER YOUR EX

Stop thinking they were a waste of time. If you learned nothing from being with them, you're the one who wasted time.

Stop comparing new loves to them, you'll give your new interest too much credit for being a decent human being, while fueling your anger for your ex.

Think about what your ex did that benefited you rather than hurt you, even in the sense they created something bad that you came out better because of it.

Believe if they wronged you, that it's karma's job to give them what they deserve – not yours.

Remember you loved or truly cared for them once and that they drove a part of you, they made you smile, fawn, daydream. Whether you'd like to admit it, accept it or not – they were a part of you. Without them, you would not be who you are today with the knowledge you have right now. They were either a blessing, a lesson, for a reason or a season. But they were crucial to the path of creating yourself.

Remind yourself things fall apart so better things can fall together.

I felt how remorselessly you hurt me
and I still wanted to love you,
to care for you,
to let you beat me up
just so you could muster a smile
in sick satisfaction.
I hopelessly ached for your happiness
and I surrendered my own
           all for you

To love or not to love

Whether we would like to admit it, our judgement in love is not always admirable. It's very blind and sometimes gets us into trouble. So you are often pleasantly surprised when someone has made the right blind choice loving you.

I, on the other hand, fear when people love me. I fear that they expect something of me that I can never return. I fear that they expect something of me that I would not return. I am unprepared to love them back and I never do, often times because they are not the kind of person I could love.

The people I love and the ones who love me are from different worlds. The ones who love me, are in relationships with other women, with themselves, with sports, with video games, with a thrill. They are in love with a fraudulent form of reality in which they believe they can have whatever they want. They believe that I should demean my beliefs to suit theirs. They turn me into someone I hate, just so they can enjoy the reflection looking back at them.

And in the world of the ones I love, they are kind, smart and capable of understanding the importance in human contact and conversation. They encompass the entirety of beauty as they are the definition. They – physically are extremely appealing because their mind shines outward they may be quiet at times but they have intelligence screaming to get out.

The ones who love me spend hours learning words to say to me to confuse me into thinking they are my ideal choice. They are the ones who say someone 'doesn't deserve me' with the ulterior motive to implicate they do. They are the ones who want to be with me in private, because I am not good enough to them to be addressed as their woman in public. They are the ones who want me to overlook the fact they are taken. They are the ones who want me to accept jewelery and flowers, when – if they had listened; they would know I wear one ring, and a rosary and in fact – I hate flowers. Because they remind me of the inevitability of our demise. They are the ones who don't know that I write... somehow.

The ones who 'claim' to love me, don't know a thing about me. So I'm sick of hearing that fucking word.

Don't ever be sorry

Don't ever be sorry for wanting a strong relationship or cute morning texts and general respect before being loured into the bed of a person who has no better intentions than *doing you right*. Don't be sorry for wanting something genuine, for the love making to come along with time or at least passion. Don't be sorry for saying no to someone who only likes you when you say yes. Don't be sorry for keeping your legs closed and your eyes open. Don't be sorry for being smart enough to know when you two want different things. Don't be sorry for wanting a real-ationship. Don't be fucking sorry for knowing you deserve better. Ever.

"Why are you so sad?"

He asked

"Because I am so unfulfilled" The words left her lips quietly, "Because I haven't lived"

"Well, why haven't you?"

"I don't know how. All I know is unhappiness"

"Well that is a part of living"

"It is?"

"Yes, the hurt. The emptiness at times.." He stepped towards her, "But there is more than that and you don't need to travel the world to find it"

He looked into her curious eyes and wondered if this would only bring trouble. If his lips pursing towards hers was the finest mistake he's ever made. If opening her eyes to the love that has been waiting years to be reciprocated. If this, right now would ruin her because she could no longer run away. If this was a lip-sealed commitment to him and not the realm of the life she could have abroad. Was he taking away her choice? All he knew was regardless of the outcome, he was handing her a piece of life – she hadn't yet lived.

THE WORST KIND OF LOVE

Do you know what the worst kind of love is equivalent to? Being addicted to drugs.

Craving something so deeply, so passionately when it couldn't be worse for you. When it couldn't be more dangerous, destructive and corrosive. Love is both amazing and stupid. Rewarding and thieving. Liberating and stifling. Love, is a drug.

The worst kind of love though, is loving someone who is totally wrong for you. The one who doesn't love you back, or doesn't treat you right, or who you don't deserve or who doesn't deserve you. The worst kind of love is the love you depend on like a crutch. The worst kind of love is the one you expect to be there for you just because you feel like the victim. We all can choose to be a victim or we can choose to be the survivor.

The worst kind of love, the worst kind of lover... is the one who can't make you see you are able to stand on your own. The worst kind of love, the worst kind of lover is the one who isolates you from family, friends, life and knowledge. The worst kind of love, the worst kind of lover is the one who demeans you and makes the worthlessness you already felt for yourself seem more significant and true. The worst kind of love, the worst kind of lover is one who makes you forget what you're capable of.

The worst kind of love, the worst kind of lover, the worst kind of love-style – is one that doesn't feel lovely at all.

THAT ONE NIGHT IN SUMMER

"Are you just going to pretend like you didn't hear what I said?" She cried.

"I heard you, okay. I don't know what to say." I responded as I continued pacing around the room.

"Whatever. Forget it."

"I–"

"When someone tells you they love you, you say something back. I love you too, maybe, or as much as it hurts – I don't love you. You can't just push me away like I'm nothing."

I don't know what it was, her news, the drugs, or just seeing my best friend cry to me but I broke. She loved me, and I couldn't feel the same. It tore me up, and I felt myself fall into a million shards of guilt. Everything in me, wanted to feel what she felt for me, for her. I didn't want our friendship to change, and I knew though after this it would. I knew she could not pretend that this night never happened, nor could I.

"I'm so sorry. I'm sorry I don't feel that way. I'm just... I'm sorry" I said as I stepped toward her to hug her.

"No." She pushed passed me. I could tell by her face her tears began to hurt, "It's okay, ya know. I get it... I actually and honestly... get it. I don't really, you know – care. I'm young. I'll find love. Someone will love me."

She left the room and I could feel our bond become frail and dissolve at the seams. The further she walked away the more my heart ached. I felt like loving her would be the easy way out, to make her happy maybe. But could I jeopardize my own happiness?

I was more surprised than anyone, when things had seemingly gone back to normal. I really feel that, because she loves me – she let it go. But I also feel, because there is so much she had not let go, that she loved me. I never wanted to add myself to the list of people that hurt her, and I guess in a way that's what made that night so hard. I do love her. Maybe not in the way she would like, but I love her the only way I can.

THE EDGE

It scares me when I push people to the edge with the way I act like I just don't care. I get weak under how they become weak. I become guilty for being the reason someone doesn't want to live.. to breathe. I'm scared because I always fall for broken people and I just don't want to be the one who breaks them for good. So I stay. I always stay. With my broken mind, broken spine I find it in me, to be strong for them. I find it in me to live with being unhappy, so they can know happiness. I guess, I save them in a way before it's inevitable that they will be broken. It can't work forever, and I know that. I'm still trying to learn how not to let my conscience be affected by letting someone go. But it hurts to know, I could be the one who pushes them to the edge.

"Baby, I'm sorry!" She wrapped herself in a sheet and ran towards Alex, blocking his way as he tried to leave.

"Get out of my face. I'm not above hitting you." Alex's jaw clenched angrily. Jennifer remained in his way. "If you don't want me to smack the shit out of you, you will move. Right now."

"No. Hit me then! Hit me if it means you're staying, please"

Alex looked down at her pleading eyes. He felt aggravated as everything built inside of him and he shoved her out of the way. He darted towards the door as he grabbed a pack of smokes off the counter and stepped outside.

His anger turned into bursts of tears that he used his palms to wipe from his face. He shook as he struggled to get his cheap lighter to work. But he relaxed as he heard footsteps nearing the front door from the inside of the house and he managed to get a spark and play it cool. *Remember you control what you do, no one else*, he thought to himself. *Not always*, he smugly argued back.

As this half naked woman who was just in his bed with his girlfriend rushed out of the house, she barely looked back before jumping in her car. *She's a home-wrecker, don't let her leave*, he thought again. Alex took a few puffs of the cigarette and tossed it on his front step and he skipped over to the car. He knocked on the passenger window and the woman looked nervously over at him and slightly wound down the window.

"Look, I'm not mad with you, it's Jen I'm mad at. I can't stand her right now. Do you think you could just give me a ride to my brothers?" Alex questioned sweetly.

Although a strange request, the woman unlocked the door and agreed. I guess she felt she owed Alex something for sleeping with his girlfriend. As they neared the address that Alex gave the woman, she grew suspicious. It was a dark road and there were very few houses, in fact none of them seemed lived in.

A small dark chuckle came over Alex and the woman looked at her options. There were very few. Alex lit up a cigarette as he winced through the front windshield, he reached in his jacket and flipped open his switch blade. Her knuckles became white as she tightened her grip on the wheel. He glared over at her with a smirk.

"Please, don't. I'll do anything" She begged, tears already welling up in her eyes.

"I hate when people beg. Does it ever really work? I'm curious.

Go ahead, beg again"

"L-l-look I'm sorry," She began hyperventilating "I didn't know she had a boyfriend. *P-please*, oh god I'm so sorry"

She's lying! Alex pushed, *this whore thinks she can just get away with what she did? Do it. DO IT NOW!* Alex pushed his blade slowly through the fabrics of her shirt until he felt it began to break through her skin. *Turn her inside out!* Anger covered his face and he punched the blade into her torso 12 times until her painful screams stopped.

With a sense of satisfaction Alex got out of the car and began walking home. No one would be sure whatever happened to that woman, or why. Though, *Jennifer might be the one who winds up dead if she cheats again*, Alex told himself, he was scared to argue back.

YOU COULD BE NEXT

I'm starving. Will I ever see daylight again? It feels like months since I've been here, though I'm pretty sure it's only been a couple of weeks. It was funny, before I felt I would die from being so scared to be in a confined space. Now, I just wish I would die. I'm cold, I'm wet, I smell. I haven't seen another human face in so long. I miss my mum. I guess you really find out who you love the most when you're away from them, and may possibly never see them again. I just miss my mum. I miss her and I miss being home in my fucking stupid little room that I complained about. I'm so ungrateful. My dad was right. I didn't see what I had and now I don't have anything..

"Let me out of here, please!" I weakly screamed. "Who are you?"

They had never responded before, why would they now? I shut up. As the silence haunted me I uneasily settled back into my thoughts. I wondered some more and realized I must've thought about every single thing on earth there was. Including the fact my family was dirt poor and they were most likely not holding me for ransom.

Just then I heard footsteps near the door of the small room I was in. I even saw a sliver of light beneath the door which helped me discover where it actually was in the pitch black. The foot steps stopped in front and created a shadow and I heard a heavy metal bar of some sort that appeared to be holding the door shut, slide open. As they pulled the door open the light blinded me and I saw the shadow of what appeared to be a tall bulky man.

As my eyes adjusted to the light the man reached for my hand and I grabbed it. He pulled me to my feet. Before I was brought here I use to watch a lot of crime shows and they say to always cooperate. Don't allow the criminal to know you are thinking of escaping or plotting anything against them. Act weak. As we stepped into the hallway of what appeared to be a gloomy old-timey wine cellar I followed him and he guided me into another corridor.

A waft of bitter, stale air smacked me in the face and as we peered around the corner through another metal door, the sight in front of me made me feel ill. The cold steel floor stung my feet and from the ceiling hung slaughtered animals. On the left hung animal carcasses, and on the right... Body parts. Human body parts. The acids in my empty stomach came hurling from my mouth and I fell weak to the ground as the man hurried me along. I screamed as I tried to resist and I screamed as I realized this was it for me. No squirming, no smooth talking, no FBI agents were going to burst through that door in the nick of time, and certainly no running – as my legs were limp as noodles – would get me out of here. He was going to kill me.

"PLEASE!" I cried, "What do you want from me?!"

He ignored my cries as he began grabbing me by my hair and pulled me up onto a steel table and he held my neck between a heavy clamp and began to walk away. No matter how hard I tugged I was stuck. My tears streamed into my ears as I fussed but I could still hear his foot steps and I dreaded for what came next.

Just kill me quickly. Please don't torture me. Just. End. It. Make this end.

And just like that… it did.

WHEN IT'S TIME TO MOVE ON

You run out of excuses for their actions. You no longer believe that someone who really loves you back could treat you this way. Your diluted daydreams no longer weigh heavier than the nightmares of your waking life. You can't lie to yourself anymore. You're in love. They are not. You need them. They don't need you.

You feel emptier the more you give to feel whole. You realize it's not getting better, and it wont. Your fear of being alone has defeated you. It has made you settle to the simplest of interactions with this person. Even a fight. Even a made up story about something they would care about because you feel it would suffice if for a moment they had interest in something you had to say.

You cry more than you laugh. You preserve memories more than make new ones. You can't say how you truly feel. Hurt. Unwanted. Alone. Minuscule. Hollow. You're conflicted between fighting and giving up on yourself. You blame yourself for not being enough for them. You blame the entire fall on your complete incompetence. You feel hopeless.

It's time to move on when, you wake up wondering why you did. You don't want to breathe, because of how useless they make you feel. When you've forgotten why people want to be in love. When you've forgotten how it felt to be alive. But it is most necessary to move on, when they've moved on from you.

I FUCKED YOU FOR THE WRONG REASON

I've been able to make you cum
    since the first day we met
    or didn't meet
    the first day we sexted.
    It was effortless to me,
    it was nothing
    to me.
    I think that
    when we met
    and I made you cum again
    it was better,
    'cause you made me cum too
    but then,
    it stopped being enough
    because I kept making you cum
    and cumming for you
    and I kept coming back.
    But when you left me alone,
    I realized the issue was, I made you want to cum,
    not want to come,

        home.

INSANE

Her fixed stare on him could have burned a whole through his flesh. Preemptively she had thought that drinking might succumb her desire to rip his head off. Rather it amplified and she found it to be a great challenge not to do so. His once piercing green eyes that reminded her of the habitat deep within a rainforest, now reminded her of destruction, gluttony, and screamed can't-be-trusted.

Smugly he lingered over to her and struck up small talk. He teased her in attempt to butter her up. A smile crossed her face artificially and you could see the satisfaction beaming out of him. Her batted lashes and poised stance loured him into a bedroom and he followed her willingly. The stench of alcohol emanated from his parted lips as he leaned in for a kiss and she pushed him back onto the bed.

As she pulled his belt off she gently put it around his neck. *Kinky*, he thought. He reached his hands for her chest and began caressing her breasts excitedly. She glared at him and then for a moment let herself enjoy it. Closing her eyes pretending it was someone worth fucking. His fingers reached beneath her dress and her eyes shot open and she looked at his smirk.

Her head tilted with a blank expression and she slowly tightened the belt around his neck. The expression on his face went from intrigue to confusion in only a few moments when he struggled to breathe. She jabbed her knee into his chest as she leaned back with the belt tightly gripped between her palms. He clawed at her firmly placed legs trying to wriggle free.

His eyes became large and filled with fear, a flame could nearly be seen within them. He was going where he belonged. Before he died she wondered does he remember her? Does he remember what he did to her, 4years-3months-10days-1hour and 16minutes ago?

She watched his life fade away in the grip of this leather noose. It didn't feel right. His face was turning purple and she saw the same look of fear and numbness that must have once crossed her own face. She let go of the belt and stepped off of him. He coughed and choked back in his life. He looked at her distraught, he did remember her, even her name, but what he never knew, was that he made her insane.

When the Hand on Your Thigh
Feels Like a Sin

When your discomfort meddles it's way in,
when your conscious takes physical form
and the voices in your head
that normally collide, combine
when the goosebumps, the chills – hurt
when the knowledge you are desired is bittersweet
when you just wish you could go back three seconds ago
when your knees weren't touching,
your eyes weren't locked
your heart was still beating
your thoughts still intact
when the hand on your thigh feels like that –
get up, don't look back.

Going cold

I wasn't sure if I had completely given up on my humanity. I'm never really sure. Every time I thought I had gone cold someone would show up, and I fell for the way they would say my name. I got chills when they would touch me, I found myself caring for them and my heart skipped several beats at a time reminding me I will always be human. Just my luck. Though, other times when I would be faced with life threatening situations, I was so calm I could have been in a coma. In these times I would watch other people completely go to shit and I couldn't figure out why they're all so damn scared to die? News flash, we are dying. The second you are born you are dying. Living is what's scary. Love is scary. Love makes me feel so numb sometimes I try to pinch myself to wake up.

But today was an insufferable amount of numbness, as though I had nova cane veins. These thoughts sped through my mind as I sat at my desk. I was itching to feel anything, and as I slid my tongue between my teeth I slowly bit down. As my rage of the emptiness I couldn't seem to escape, and the lifestyle I could no longer endure – built, I bit down harder. I bit down harder until my jaw locked into place and it seemed only ruins of my tongue remained. As a bath of blood left my tongue and streamed down my chin I realized what I had just done. Not because I felt it, and not because it hurt – but rather because it covered the page of my textbook and I was snapped out of my daze. I do not feel anymore alive than I had ten minutes before.

As my classmates noticed the blood pour onto my desk I saw their blurred figures run for paper towels and the phone for the nurse. A few of them even used their own clothing as they held it onto my destroyed tongue. I stared down as their sweaters and paper towels became red, and I began to wonder why the blood hasn't stopped yet. Blood had always made me feel uneasy and the more that transpired from my now pulsing tongue the more faint I felt. I fell out of my seat and the cold tile floors accommodated me. My screaming classmates worried chatter faded as I heard only my heartbeat and as I felt it painfully slow, I realized if life is not numb – it hurts.

Just
let me
become
unconscious
for a while,
or many whiles
until the while
exceeds a return,
and the doctor
pulls the plug

WINNIE

"I'm tired."
Winnie said as she placed her face in her palms.

"Why don't you just get in a nap?"
Eleanor responded as her expression filled with concern.

"No. I mean, I'm tired of being here. I feel like I don't have anyone."

"You have me, Hun"
Eleanor smiled sweetly.

"Yeah, I know. Thanks"

Winnie smiled back, knowing that a 50 year old woman she spoke to at work, wouldn't make a difference. In fact, Winnie became even more discouraged as she spoke to this woman who seemed to be the only one who was willing to be her friend.

She had always felt that, no one understood her. Her friends had always been inarticulate or just obsessed with a lifestyle that she would never fit into. She just loved having friends and having things to do. She kept herself busy. Now that her friends were gone it was the first time in years she had to do stuff on her own. Not realizing that, the whole time she had 'friends' she had been going at the world alone anyways. Anywhere her friends had asked her to be, she'd been there, even though sometimes she would be ridiculed. She made excuses for their behavior. When they wouldn't show up places that she wanted, she told herself somehow, she was at fault.

She even managed to fall into a drug haze where she spent weeks at a time high off of anything she could get her hands on. She needed an escape from the people that she naïvely believed she needed around her. Though as she was doped up and her hallucinations were still too close to reality she realized, her outlet was failing and her pain was too deep.

Winnie was past the drug phase in her life, but she stood there finding it more difficult to hold back her honest emotions. Winnie untied her change belt, grabbed her bag and ran out of work. She sprinted around the corner as her boss called after her and she kept running until she was out of view. She looked back as she continued walking at a fast pace.

Her chest rose and fell beneath her thoughts as she pushed into her house. She entered her room and dropped her bag to the floor. She frantically dug through the clutter pushed beneath her bed until she found what she was looking for. A bag full of pills that she had hidden there months ago, she stared at them intently before ripping the bag open; more than a dozen falling to the floor. Her shaking hand flung a handful in her mouth and she looked around for water to ease them down. One by one the pills glided brashly down her throat.

Her eyes fluttered before rolling back revealing none of her forest green iris. She laid back and examined the junk she had pulled from beneath her bed. She found notes that she somehow felt worth keeping, and pictures of memories worth remembering, and as she saw the faces of her best friends she cringed. Why don't they care about me? She thought as she begun to hallucinate.

The pictures began to move and the memories played in front of her. She remembered that time she laughed so hard she peed herself in front of them. They still brought it up three years later. She smiled faintly. The time they were lost in the woods and lost almost everything they owned but still made it into a journey they would always appreciate. Her smile stretched ear to ear as she settled in a dream.

"WINNIE!? Oh my God, Frank! Call an ambulance!!" Her mother screamed as she saw her daughter lie still on the floor.

"Honey!! Are you okay!? Oh m— Oh my god. Her eyes.. they're white! Honey!! Hurry up she's dying!!"

She faintly heard her dads panicked footsteps and shaking voice on the phone as her mother tugged her into her lap.

"Mommy?"
She muttered.

"Yes honey!? I'm here, I'm here honey, it's me!" Her mother choked out her words.

"I'm tired."

Winnie's eyes peaked out before her lids became heavy and closed one last time.

DON'T FALL IN LOVE WITH SOMEONE
WHO DOESN'T LOVE THEMSELVES;

Unless you want to turn ugly to beauty with the simple act of being present. Being available emotionally and physically. Unless you understand the difference between when they're fishing for compliments and when they really just don't see what you see. Don't fall in love with someone who thinks it's a cruel joke when someone says 'I love you'.. unless you are ready to be a reminder that it's true and unless you're prepared to say it and mean it when you do. Don't fall for their insecurities and how they're silent in a crowd. Don't fall for the way they shine when you've done something that means the world to them. Don't fall in love with their gratefulness over things that weren't enough for people in your past. Don't fall for them, when you finally hear them laugh. Don't fall for their sadness, and how it makes art. Don't fall for the wounds on their arms that tear them apart to look at. Whatever you do; don't fall in love with someone who doesn't love themselves unless you'll help them learn to.

LOSING YOURSELF

You don't ever get moments in bliss when you fuck up. The consequences are almost simultaneous.

You know in your subconscious what you're doing or what you're about to do is wrong, but your emptiness converts itself into reason; and so you do the wrong thing to gain the right feelings.

Little do you know, you become more and more lost, to the point beyond recognition. You forget who you are, what you stand for, what you love.

You forget everything until your subconscious fades into a silence that you think you'll never hear again, and then soon, the only result is consequences.

Losing people you love, becoming someone you hate, losing your decency and everything you were respected for, you lose the part of you that *is* you. You're just lost, and you don't know where you're going.

REMEMBER ME

Remember me
when my last breath
has expired.

Remember me,
when my lifeless body,
no longer heals my scars

as this time
they've punctured me
much too deep.

Remember me,
for the times I
put you ahead of me

Remember me,
for my efforts
to be better

remember me,
for the things I did
to make you smile

as I couldn't
ever give this gift
to myself.

Remember me,
six feet under,
as I finally rest

remember me,
enclosed in a coffin
of English Oak

Remember me,
as someone who
always tried to care,

as I found
myself caring,
far too deeply for you.

Would you just,
remember me?

LISALLY AND CLARKE

"Okay, it's filming" She smiled as she focused her camera on him.

"What should I do?"

"Anything. Talk about yourself."

"You really want to be a reporter, huh. Okay, I'm Clarke. I'm friends with Lisally's older brother. I hope to be—"

"Clarke," Lisally noticed two figures walking up behind Clarke in the lens. "Behind you"

Clarke's focus didn't move from Lisally's direction as he noticed another approaching behind her and Clarke stepped to her in one motion shielding her from the oncoming men. Before any words were spoken mischievous smirks crossed all three of their faces. In panic Lisally gripped the back of Clarke's Jacket breathing heavy into his back.

"Hey there beautiful" One of the men said tauntingly, "We're just here to make friends. I'm Allan, and you?"

Still skeptical she answered politely but Clarke didn't speak a word he could see their intentions in the way they would look her up and down.

"Lisally, that's a pretty name. Can I tell you something, Lisally?" She nodded faintly, "Come here"

"No." Clarke had a death grip on Lisally's wrist.

"Oh come on." Allan continued to toy with them, "I just want to let her in on a little something"

Allan stepped toward Lisally and Clarke jumped in the way giving Allan a shove.

"What do you want?"

"Oh, we've got a tough guy here" Allan said as he looked back at his chuckling friends. "Boys."

On his cue his friends restrained Clarke leaving Lisally nervously standing unprotected. Allan crept towards her as she stared at the pavement uncomfortably. She felt his rough and tattered hands run up her shaking back. He placed greasy kisses on her neck as she tried to turn from them without seeming too disobedient, as she didn't know what they would do. Clamped in her hands she held her camera still on record.

Clarke tried to fight free of the hands of whom seemed to be Allan's sidekicks as he struggled to watch what was about to happen to his best friends little sister. Not to mention the girl he just started seeing as a young woman. He saw Allan walk her over to a nearby parked car as he bent her over the hood holding her arms roughly behind her back. He reached around her waist and began unfastening his belt and then paused.

"Ay, one of you got a condom?" He called over to his sidekicks.

They chuckled as one reached into his pockets loosening the grip on Clarke's arm and Clarke used the opportunity to wriggle free and threw a punch with his free arm and then swung at the other. He darted toward Allan but caught himself off guard feeling his own hand break against Allan's jaw.

Allan's teeth clenched angrily as he turned towards Clarke and shoved him to the ground while pulling out a gun tucked into the waist of his jeans he aggressively pointed it at him. Clarke put up his hands now fearing what would happen to Lisally.

"Wait! Stop!" Lisally screamed

Her scream was echoed by a gunshot and she stared at Clarke's wounded torso begin to bleed. As she noticed Allan get ready to shoot again she forced out another scream.

"I've recorded everything!" She moved the camera around as she got all of their faces clearly on screen. "He's going to bleed out.. I'm the real threat now.. Catch me unless you want to go to jail for murder"

"Lisy run!" Clarke forced out.

One of the side kicks stomped on Clarke's chest to shut him up.

Lisally had already sprinted off into the darkness and all three of them chased after her. She ran through neighborhood watch surveilled blocks in hopes someone might be able to help her. She ran in between two houses as she heard the skipping feet of them running the streets. She panted silently as she tried to catch her breath while she hid.

Just as she relaxed she felt a tug and she was thrown to the ground by her hair. She heard the familiar grunts and chuckles of Allan and his posse as her face was down in the gravel. Allan kicked her in her face and the tips of his shoes were trailed with her blood.

"Don't ever make me run." He said with a much meaner tone.

He spat at her as she quietly cried into the gravel until they all began to kick her ribs and stomp on her back. Her cries became louder and the sound of her spitting and coughing out blood were the only noises she could make.

"Now give me the fucking camera."

He roughly rolled her over onto her back and dug through her jacket until he found it and shoved it into his pocket.

"Now, where were we?"

He roughly tugged at the waist of her pants as she screamed. He put his hand over her mouth as he dug his fingers deep into her cheeks until he could feel the grooves of her teeth.

"Shut the fuck up. If you scream again I swear, I will kill you." Lisally's hands fell helplessly to her sides. But her heart raced as she felt a large rock skim beneath her palm. Before Allan could get her pants down she swung the rock over his head and he fell to the ground beside her. Lisally jumped to her feet and darted away.

"FUCK!" Allan wailed as he held his pounding forehead. "Jesus Christ that fucking hurt!"

"Man, you okay? Should we go get her??"

"No, forget it! I could barely look at that bitches face with all that damage. We got the camera we're good."

"Alright bro."

Allan dusted himself off and wiped the blood from his forehead on his sleeve. He muttered to himself. He dug into his pocket for the camera as he went to look at the face of the girl that outsmarted him. He grew enraged as his eyes stalled on the screen of her camera.

"Clarke?" She cried "Please don't be dead."

"Lisally.. Your face.." He muttered

"Oh my g— You're alive. We have to go, come on, we have to go. Can you stand?"

Lisally helped Clarke to his feet and they limped all the way to the police station. Officers surrounded the two of them with concern and Lisally handed an officer the memory card from her camera.

YOU'RE LONELY

Admit it. Nights you feel it the most, you turn restlessly in your sheets as if you were banned from sleep. You can't close your eyes to dreams, they've been rewritten. You open the blinds to a sunny sky, that just seems wasted; it seems grey. You feel like nothing and no one can put soul back into you. Your heart doesn't even beat anymore. You're programmed to smile and laugh on cue. You realized you have been consumed with a bitterness that grows. You lose it. You begin to lie to yourself, say that you are happy with your life. You say you are content, that you don't need a relationship to be happy. You say you'd rather not have friends than have friends who betray you. You say that your life is just how you want it, and eventually… Eventually you have broken down each sensical bone in your body until you collapse under your lies, that you are okay. When that is not the case. You get to the point where you believe you are better, you believe you are over feeling like no one wants you, no one needs you. But really, you've just hidden the reason you were sad, but you weren't strong enough to actually cease the sadness. You remain lost. You have this rotting hole that gets bigger that becomes an emptiness. People look in your eyes and even they can tell, nobody lives there. You're lonely, admit it.

my emotions are dead
filling up empty space
while being absolutely
useless.

every time I smile,
I wonder if it's real.
or whether it's just polite
not to waste others time.

not even tears
exist to me anymore
the corpse of my emotion –
breathless

TWO MINUTES

You have
two minutes
to cry
say *fuck you,*
goodbye.

Two minutes
to forget
have not a thing
to regret.

Two minutes
to bask in the reality
that you aren't perfect
that you aren't 'her'
you aren't 'the one'
that you aren't invincible
you aren't living to your full potential
you aren't special
— you just aren't.

Two minutes
to admit you're a slob
you leave your table etiquette at home
you talk too much
you're a bit of a loner
and you're extremely strange
— you just are.

you have
two minutes –
1:59
        1:58 …

My fear saved my life

instinct
loaded the gun,
fear
removed the bullets

pain,
tied the knot,
fear
cut me down.

hurt,
swallowed the pills,
fear
purged them up.

alive,
because of fear.
dead *inside,*
because of you

ABC ALLITERATION CHRONICLES

aggravated punches puncture her skin,
    black and blue bruises arise from within
    caught in a formidable fight, she can't win
    dangerous lands lay, if she stays with him.

everything ignites in her it's insane,
    fallen faint to a frivolous flame,
    got caught caring 'bout a cowardly frame
    hopelessly hoping he leaves from her brain.

in desperate pleas of purposeful prayers,
    just trying to tie up time until someone is there
    knowing only a small sacred second is to spare
    losing more beats and breaths than she can bare

mutilating her hurting heavy soul,
    not sure if her locked lips'll let go
    of the loveless lust he lacked to show
    poured it all, let her fenced fears flow..

quietly bleeding bliss-less pain
    real eyes, realizing, real lies once tamed,
    so, solemnly stuck in wasted shame
    to moments that made her a maid to her name

under the impression it'd impress him
    vacant of the thought time wouldn't progress him
    wondering where and when she would've left him
    x-raying the corruption of her chests last possession

      young yet she seemed as though she lost sense of her heart.
      zig zagging around an asshole that allowed her to forget –

      She was art.

Sexually

frustrated people

chew on ice.

Emotionally,

frustrated people

chew on cement

until they can't talk

and their whole body

has gone numb,

until their organs

have clogged

and their brain

has stopped

and their hearts

last beat

beats,

through

    concrete.

THE ONLY WAY I'LL LEAVE

Treat me like I don't exist, give me a kiss, with a fist. Treat me like I'm no one, pull the trigger on your gun you threaten me with. Penetrate me with the knife you've threatened to decapitate me with. Follow through on your threats, and all the things you said you would do, if I looked at anyone else the way I look at you. Because the only way I'll be through with you is if I'm feet beneath the ground you've thrown me to. It's crazy that I'm determined to be with a monster, you're the worst thing for me, but – kill me; it's the only way I'll leave.

LA TOILE DEMONS

She was Satan's canvas, and his paint brush was a blade,
he drew her inevitable death in different crimson shades.
The digs were sometimes shallow, but 'times it was made
deep enough that the next dig, would also be her grave.

She couldn't look in the mirror because she did not exist,
she use to be the beauty that art would sometimes miss.
She was always happy, she was the pleasure in a kiss,
she took the chaos and gave her loved ones bliss.

But she was in a chokehold, she couldn't stand the fight,
Satan's masterpiece was finished, and he finally took her life.

Did you taste my blood when you kissed me,
    from the cuts along my lip?
    The taste of my dried out words,
    that escape my finger tips?

Did you feel how I pushed away,
    when you held me in your grasp?
    I forgot what happiness was
    I forgot when I felt it last.

Do you remember why and when,
    I began to run from you?
    You were too daft to see,
    what was fake and what was true.

So I did what it took,
    to get away from hell.
    I tied a noose around my neck,
        and I killed myself.

IN THE MORNING

I remember the late nights that turned into mornings, and I remember the security I had with you guys next to me, and the sunrise behind me. I could finally rest, and relax. The way I couldn't rest or relax in the paranoia of the night. I remember coming home when the sun found a few moments between the car and my back door to taint my skin. I remember being in a comfortable empty house, since it was daylight. I slept for but a few hours and I remember waking up and staying up until that night so we can leave again and return in morning... when I was comfortable enough to sleep, *for a while*.

Annie and Brent

His eyes lingered across the room and he watched her nervously pick at her nails. She was in her own head and he could tell it was hell in there. He didn't know how to comfort her the way he wanted to from the opposing side of the room.

"I'm worried about you"

"You shouldn't be. I'm fine." she said beneath her breath as she had long waited for him to say something.

"You're not eating. You think you're so imperfect but you're beautiful and amazing and–"

"Listen, you don't have to worry about me I'm not trying to fit into societies perfect image."

"Exactly, you're trying to fit into your own and I know you. Nothing you've ever done has been good enough for you. You're never satisfied. It scares me because I know one day you're going to take yourself away from me and how many times can I say that you are perfect to me until you believe me and maybe you feel the same way about yourself. God dammit, Annie!" He slammed his clenched fists on his desk and she jumped, "I need you."

"You don't need me, Brent. You just thi–"

"Don't tell me what I need. Annie, I have loved you for eight years." She paused and it seemed like she just began to listen, "No, not as my friend. I love you like I want you to be my wife! I get that you're not into me like that, fine. I can stand living by your side as your best friend that you wont think of as anything more, ever. But if you continue losing yourself.. I think I'll die."

Annie stood up and walked towards Brent as he had his face in his palms. She sat next to him and grabbed his fork and began picking food off his plate. He looked up as he pushed the tears off of his face and he smiled from the corner of his mouth. Annie smiled as she chewed like it was her first time and they both laughed. He looked at her as he felt his heart become light. She hugged him and placed a kiss on his cheek that quite frankly he was okay with if it didn't mean anything.

They found their way to the couch and as time passed Brent began to doze off. The ease of their break through put him to sleep like a baby. Annie waited for a moment for the security of his snores and she gently pushed herself up. She tip toed to the bathroom. She closed the door behind her as she turned on the tap to drain the noise. She put her fingers deep to the back of her throat and just like that, she had her control.

161

GREG AND LYNNE

I feel when people step aside into another room your curiousness of it all will breach the privacy that those people, whom by leaving the room, were trying to reach. As a young girl I always felt that the best stories were the ones that were overheard. I found out amazing little secrets that I selfishly sometimes used to get a later bedtime or dessert without eating my vegetables. But sometimes the things meant to be unseen and unheard uncovered something deep. I felt that the truest side of a person was revealed when they believed to be in private.

Every morning my mom would wake me up with a little jingle. My favorite things were how she sang me awake and to sleep. She seemed like the happiest, sweetest woman on earth. So when I would sometimes come home after school and hear my mom crying in her room, I felt sick. After the first time I began to sneak into the house just to see if she was crying again, and she always was.

I asked my dad one day why mom was sad and his disinterest in the subject made me believe he was already aware and annoyed of the situation. Shortly after I initially asked I remember for the first time hearing my parents fight. My dad yelled at my mother as he explained that she was worrying me. I felt comfort in the fact he was concerned about how I was being affected but confused in the way he went about it.

I never once felt inconvenienced by my mothers sadness, I was concerned more than anything. Though, I assumed if she had not cried in front of me then it was not yet time for me to ask.

One evening I was woken out of bed as I heard something shatter against their bedroom floor the next room over. I remember noticing on my clock it was after 1AM, and this was the fourth day this week my dad had come in late.

I sat up in my bed wondering if I should interrupt their arising dispute. I stayed in bed a little longer as my eyes dilated in the dark with only the hall light beneath my door. I pushed the sheets off of me as I moved my feet around to find the part of my floor not covered in clothes and toys and I tip toed to the door. I turned my knob with expertise making sure I didn't make a sound and I slickly slipped into the hall.

As I neared my parents bedroom and the shouted words became more clear I gently placed my ear to the door and awaited some clarity to the situation.

"..I can't do this anymore, Greg." I heard my mothers voice

proclaim.

"Do what?"

"THIS. It was one thing to find out you were having an affair in the first place, but now to know you haven't stopped.."

I remember my obliviousness to the word 'affair' so nothing yet really peaked my interest aside from my parents rising voices.

"I cheated because you stopped treating me like your husband!"

"You only think that because we stopped having sex."

I shied from the door as my cheeks went red, this was one of the most embarrassing but intriguing conversations I had heard at this age.

"I am sick, Greg!"

"That isn't my fault!" My dad yelled back.

There was a long pause for my mothers response and I wondered if they had perhaps heard me at the door, but just as I went to back away I heard my mothers voice.

"No Gregory. It isn't your fault that I have terminal cancer. It isn't your fault that our daughter is going to lose her mother. It isn't your fault that I can't fuck you god dammit because I'm in pain twenty-four hours of the entire fucking day!" My jaw dropped at the words that escaped my mothers tongue, "But it *is* your fault that you didn't have the decency to leave the marriage rather than cheat on a dying woman."

Dying. That word chilled my bones. I felt sick again and my legs carried me through the hall as I flung into the bathroom and hunched over the toilet to puke. I puked up nothing but acid as I held on to my aching stomach. My mom came running out of their room and knelt next to me concerned as she vigorously rubbed my back and my dad stood vacant at the door.

It was then I wondered if he realized what was happening. Certainly my father could not have willfully neglected the woman he had been with for twenty years, especially if he knew she wouldn't be here much longer.

I tried to stop vomiting long enough to speak to my mother as she pulled my hair out of my face.

"You're dying!" I cried out, "How could you not tell me that!?"

My mothers face went sour and she looked back at my dad and he stepped into the bathroom and sat down next to us. He hugged me tightly and I felt his clinched jaw dig into my head as I cried into his shirt and we sat there as a family for the second last time.

Looking back, I respect my parents for staying together in the last months of my mothers life for my sake. Because on top of knowing she was dying, knowing my parents were splitting up would have put my pain over the top. Surely now I do realize the meaning of all the secrets revealed that night, but what I had not known was how long my mother was suffering. So when she passed that same night in mine and my fathers arms I realized she was in a better place.

The following sunday we attended the funeral for my mother, Lynne. That was the last time we sat together as a family. Many months following that day, my dad cried just as often and just as pain filled as my mother once had. He would cry over the pictures of them. He loved her the way he always had, and mentally I believe his affair stopped the day my mother died. I wasn't sure up until I understood what an affair was, to decide initially if I was upset with my father, and then to see how much he hurt to now decide if I forgave him. I feel that the truest side of someone is revealed when they believe to be in private.

Titanic

All societal bounds
limits, classes, races
immersed, drowned
into one cold oceanic blur

Love matters more;
what you stand for
what you'll fall by

Just as my heart sinks,
you flood my thoughts
I will go down, too
           with you.

I NEED YOU MORE THAN YOU NEED ME

She knocked lightly on her daughters bedroom door with her ear pressed against it. Holding her breath as she awaited a response, a voice, a grunt, anything indicating that the worst has not yet come.

"Yeah?" Her daughter responded quietly. She sighed in relief and stood there for another moment "Hello?.." Her daughter responded again.

She departed from her daughters door and slipped into her own room and choked down her tears. The way it seems like her daughter lately has craved to disappear; was her biggest fear.

ROCHELLE

"It's not you, it's m —"

"Bullshit."

"Okay. It is you." His jaw clenched "Dammit Rochelle, you always make me say things that insult you."

"What's insulting is that after ten years you can't be honest with me."

"It isn't easy for me to tell you that..."

"That you don't love me anymore.."

"Saying those words, makes me sick."

"Hearing it is no better." She winced, as she held her tears.

"It's disgusting to think you could wast– I mean spend, ten years with a person only to find out, you are so.. wrong for each other. It's cruel."

She sat there with a compressed jaw.

"So wrong" She lied.

"You feel it too?"

"I have."

"Do you think we could still be friends?"

"Of course."

She said knowing they could not and would not be friends. In fact, they just might be enemies. The one who breaks your heart becomes the villain, that you won't rest until you slay.

SKELETONS

At night I remember;
all the things the sun
scared into shaded corners

At night they pull me in;
there is no light bright enough,
no monster deflecting bed cover –
strong enough
to save me from submitting
to the taunting squeals and shrieks
of the hollowed bones
collecting in my closet

They want to be remembered
and I just want to forget

THOUGHTS THAT KEEP ME UP AT NIGHT

It's that comfort I will never experience, it's the nonchalantness of it all, that I will never get. It is what will make my past so hard to forget. I will suffocate beneath the naked fiending body that thrusts carelessly into me as I digress. When I am listless and quiet at their side I will disguise my thoughts faintly with a smile. I will listen to them brief me on their whereabouts from when my phone remained un-rung. That or..

A man crazy enough to fall for me, will love me much too deeply. He will cry when I cry; heart wrenching, painful tears that twist within the sheets. The sheets – that because of me; will banish sleep. I may just ruin his life – a man crazy enough to fall for me, because I am ruined. That or..

One day the man with eyes for me, will stop the ugly from taking over me. The man with wise words and endless hope will show me I am more than what others have demeaned me. The man will remind my hurting heart, that it will heal with time just maybe not the same. He'll remind me that I will love again, just, maybe not the same. He'll remind me that because I have seen evil that I can live right. He will remind me that I can no longer blindly let my emotions exude through my skin. I cannot be delicate glass held together by glue. I can be strong, I am strong, I don't need to shelter myself. He will remind me that I can't forget to live, I can't stop even if I just go step by step.

John & Sara

The second I answered the phone, she knew. She knew as my voice was tired that I was lying next to someone else.

She remained quiet. As we both boiled in the agonizing silence I looked to my left as the girl I just fucked; slept blissfully. The mediocre girl in bed with me would never know such pain. She would live a life of drunken weekends and 9-5 shifts while her attention was glued to her phone.

I crept out of bed as I lingered into the next room. As my ear was deafened by her silent disapproval, I opened my mouth to speak.

"I'm sorry"

"When are you coming home?" She said with no emotion.

"I can come now, if you want" I said as I glared back into the bedroom.

She paused before I heard the phone click in my ear. I tiptoed back into the room as I collected my jeans and the rest of my clothes. I cringed as I realized I coward to even have the guts to say goodbye to this girl who has probably been in this situation dozens of times. I pulled her front door in behind me, still with my clothes in my hand. I dressed in the car as I put my keys in the ignition. I shoved my sock-less feet into my shoes and combed my hair with the tips of my fingers as I glared in the rearview mirror.

The drive home felt much too quick as I pulled up my driveway. I sat in the car reluctant to get out until I noticed the front light turn on and I pulled myself together. I straightened my clothes and when I went up to the front door it was unlocked. The hall light was on and I kicked off my shoes. My heart beat sporadically as I walked down the hall. I went to our bathroom and she was in there washing her face. I said nothing and hopped in the shower. I scrubbed the fruity perfume smell off of my chest as it seemed to be seeping into my skin.

When I got out of the shower she sat in bed. She had a book in her lap and she wore the reading glasses that she knew I loved. Her legs were crossed and she had her hair in a messy bun. She didn't look up at me as I neared the bed. She was good at acting like she didn't notice the things around her. I knew she noticed me but I still craved for her attention. I would often come home and seem to forget why I left. Love shouldn't fade when you're apart, so I often doubted that's what it was. Until I was back with her again, then I knew.

I sat next to her and my weight on the bed made her fall into me. Her hands touched my leg as she pushed herself back up. I bit my lip as her big brown eyes looked up at me. She turned away and she put her book on the end table and laid on her side with her back to me. I stared for a moment and she put her hand out reaching back for me to coddle her. I didn't think twice and I swept my feet under the sheets and laid behind her. I wrapped my arms around her and she skimmed her uncertain fingers along the hairs on my arms as they stood up. I kissed the back of her head as my guilt settled in my stomach.

We laid so close but there was a distance between us that I wasn't sure could be restored. But she wanted me still, despite what I did behind closed doors.

我們都知道 你愛我

I'm sorry I threw out your poem
or maybe a several few ..
Sorry I've chosen to forget your words
and the ones I wrote for you
I don't want to read them
because now I know they were all lies
Though skimming through your stanzas
I see the goodbyes between the lines
I never read them carefully;
the words you got off your chest
But now I've paid attention
and I'm seeing all the rest
I was there only to fill holes
to carry you 'til you could walk on
Now you're whole and on your feet
and I am to be forgotten.

◆

I shouldn't
hate you
just because
you didn't love me
when I needed it
but I think
I should hate you
for pretending
like you did.

I DON'T KNOW WHAT YOU DO WHEN I'M NOT AROUND ALL I KNOW IS IT KILLS YOU

The way you look at me,
all I see in your absent auburn eyes is anguish.
You come back with black bawdy bruises,
blanketing your brittle arms.
You confide in me, in a constrained careful custom.
While drying dire discontent damp tears from your cheeks.
Everything everyone expects from you has this effect on you,
       so you escape.
I feel frightened that I too fall far from faith along with you.
That every gnawing gaping gasp you give out, is mine too.
I always watch you hurt helplessly, hoping somehow, you heal.
I imagine it's like an igniting indescribable impairment,
just jabbing your jaw to jot what your mouth won't say –
                    in your skin.
The knife-like blade keying your flesh kept keeping you kind.
Lying, like losing love didn't make you lost.
Magnificently masking your mortified marred expressions,
to avoid feeling like a nervous naïve nuisance.
I'm obsessed with opening you up to orbit over,
          around and through you.
Perhaps to peek in your past, putting puzzle pieces in place,
answering questions that quite often make you quiver
          quibbling over them.
I see the resentment, your red eyes regretfully revert,
sniffing back your sulfuric sorrows,
trying to trick tears to play hide and seek.
Unaware it was useless, as it was an uncompromising
          unending stream.
Although a very valiant attempt to stop the verge of tears,
you wore a wondrous smile as you left me waiting for your return,
          as your reflection in the mirror.
I miss when you tried, to make us feel zany, zesty and zeal
when we looked into each others eyes.

       I don't know what you do when I'm not around,
                 all I know is it kills you.

Never sleep

I use to turn over in the middle of the night and stare at you intently until I saw your chest rise and fall. You're by my side and all. But not really. I see the emptiness in your eyes and the vacancy in your voice. Like you're only staying because I gave you no choice. It's like you don't really breathe you just take in air to survive. You're not really living, and you bleed to know you're alive. I worry about you, caring about you is a promise I can keep.. And knowing you're unhappy and alone is the reason I never sleep.

EVERY WRITERS DEATH

Every writers death,
every dreamers final rest
is always a tragedy
Very few sets of eyes,
view the world
in volumes,
in endless beauty,
in metaphorical scenery,
that relates to our mood,
our thoughts,
our passion
We are the trees, leaves,
the petals,
and especially the thorns
We are the air,
and we are the absence of it
We are light,
and we are the absence of it
We are heat,
and we are the absence of it
We give the world so much life
and without us,
it is in absence of it
and so every writer,
every dreamer, every beings death
is always a tragedy.

DROWN

I grabbed your wrists,
trying to wring them
free of my neck.
The water
filled up my lungs;
Why wasn't I dead yet?

I looked
into your empty eyes,
and you smiled.
I squirmed,
helplessly in your grasp
like a newborn child.

Then I thought,
about all the times,
you knocked me down.
This was a blessing,
to finally be rid of you
and let myself drown.

BLACK INK

I've written this letter
six times,
and it's never been
just right.

I roll my pen
along the page
trying to make sense
of whats in my mind.

I'm trying to understand
why I still want you so bad..
but for some reason
it can't work.

You'll let me die
without knowing you,
the way you already
know me.

I've scribbled out my
admittance to loving you
more than I should
and replaced it with
'I just care about you'

I never get what I
really want to say out,
I don't know what
I'll need to be ready for if I do.

You're in my head.
you're in my heart ..
I'm so scared of you..
but I start my letter over
for the seventh time

Trying to explain
the depth of my love for you.
and I penetrate
the heart on my sleeve
with my pen,

and I bleed black ink
all over the page –

now it says how I feel;
just right.

MISSING

So many people missing,
    all the hearts, I hear them break
    So many tears being shed,
    feelings that they can't shake

We're all missing at some point;
    there's something unavoidable about that
    But my heart and prayers go out
    to the ones, who don't come back.

NEVER SAY NEVER

Never say never
don't ever say always.
Don't promise forever,
If you'll pass me in hallways.

Don't tell me you're staying,
that you'll never leave.
Don't say your heart is my home,
then take back the keys.

Don't ever say always,
don't ever say never,
Don't make the promise,
that we'll end up together.

SANDY

Her groans were muffled into the sheets. She crawled towards the end table as the springs dug into her knees. Squinting at the phone she read the caller ID. It was her mother. She answered and her mothers voice was unintelligible on the other end.

"Mum. Mum, slow down. What?" She asked as she tried to wake herself up, "A shooting? Bethany's school? What? What are you talking about?"

Her mother insisted she turned on the TV. There it was. An air view of her daughters school surrounded by parking lot of police and ambulances. She jumped out of bed without hanging up the phone or turning off the TV. She threw on her coat, grabbed her keys and frantically jumped in her car.

Her eyes hadn't blinked even once for what felt like the longest drive she ever endured. Her heart was practically leaping out of her chest and she could hardly breathe. Her hands were gripped so tightly on the wheel she lost pigment in her skin. She didn't want to accept the worst. Her daughter was alive — she had to be.

She pulled into the parking lot over crowded with police cars and other parents trying to fnd their child. Students were being evacuated, she looked at every brown haired little girl hoping for one to be her daughter. She ignored the screams of pain the parents who had already learned of their child's passing. She refused to accept she would ever feel that pain. She watched and waited and she was fought off by police several times asking her to stay back.

A mother from across the way who held her son tightly stared at her. She knew Bethany. Bethany was in her sons class. She caught this mothers eyes and the mother stared at her long until she gave a subtle shake of the head. She mouthed 'I'm sorry'.

"No. no.. no no no no.. no" She shook her head frantically as she fought back tears, "Bethany! Wheres my daughter? Give me my daughter. Tell her to come out!"

"Ma'am. I'm sorry if she isn't already out here.. she was one of the victims." An officer said sadly.

Her eyes welled with tears until they blinded her. She fell to her knees with her head in her hands and she stopped breathing, long enough – to die inside.

I'M DEHYDRATED

I've been drained of tears,
drained of care,
drained of all the things
you want to matter to me;
but just don't.

I'm dehydrated,
but I haven't got a thirst
for much of anything.

HER SUICIDE NOTE READ:

I don't owe any one of you a fucking explanation.

A WRITERS ENDING

And then
the gun went off,
his body collapsed
and his skull cracked
into the ground –
after that shot,
nothing else made a sound

The voices he heard
disappeared
all in that moment –
seems so sad, it had
to come to that,
don't it?

Do you get it now?

Do you feel me
beneath my skin
when you burn
a hole through it –
groping deep beneath
what I'd allow
had I learned
not to be so
transparent?

Do you feel me
ache, shake,
do you feel
what resonates
within my being?

Do you feel me,
do you get it
or do you still think
I'm a toy,
and this is all a game?

I'm tired

I'm tired of writing
about the same old thing,
The same person, the same sadness
that thinking of them brings.

I'm tired of feeling,
like this old tortured soul,
I'm tired of the fact,
I'm unable to let go.

I'm tired of dreaming,
of what we could have been,
I'm tired of nothing
being as it seems.

I'm tired of distress,
the restlessness of each day..
But mostly I'm tired of remembering,
it was *me* who walked away.

I just feel trapped.
Latched.
Arms and Legs, strapped.
Too many problems
not enough air,
any moment
my heart may collapse.
I'm stuck
life's passing too fast.
Overdose on thoughts
an in completion of tasks
When will I ever
get myself back..

Or will I die before that?

AFTER

After you fuck me
without my permission,
would you kill me this time?
Would you rid me of my memories
so I don't get out of line?
So I don't push every guy
far enough from my heart,
so I don't get the chance
to fall in love to start with?
Could you do it quickly enough,
so that I'm unable to cry?
Could you do it
so maybe,
I don't want to die?

When you fuck me again
without my permission,
       kill me this time.

THERAPY

"Why did you forgive your attacker?"

"It's how I was brought up. I was often neglected and I had to be my own parent a lot of the time. I had older siblings but they weren't around. We were so far in age nothing I wanted to go to them about would even be discussible. I grew up believing I didn't deserve very much and I have been a people pleaser ever since. I do everything, I still do — to make people happy. It makes them happy, and it is my only joy. I know that's a little pathetic but."

"So you forgave your attacker because you wanted to make them happy?...Or you didn't feel you deserved better?"

"Personally, I didn't want the problems. I'm not good at staying mad even when I have good reason. I feel weak with trying to hate people but my grandmother always said it takes someone strong to forgive. But I could never figure out why each time I was victimized, my rerunning thoughts were... 'Please don't do this, I don't want it to ruin things.' I didn't want relationships, friendships or trust to be broken over me. That's the fucked up part is I felt responsible. Neither times did I ever involve authorities because all I could think about was.. other people. To this day I have had 3 more encounters where I was victimized and it has become so — I don't know; but now I've turned it into something that it's not. I've turned it into 'they don't know what they're doing' I turn it into 'Maybe if I don't cry, then it's not rape.' I try to justify their behavior so I don't have to go through this again.. so I'm not that 16 year old girl again. So I don't have to keep guarding myself and shutting myself off from other people. I don't think it's fair that I'm like this. I'm too forgiving."

CHOKE

There's a taste when you choke
from the inside of your throat
Your tongue floats
on your saliva
and you drown in a rote
of the same shit,
the same trials,
you can't quit.

There's a taste when you choke
on the inside of your throat,
that bloat your lungs
with thick smoke
of unrequited dote
and the words
of each suicide note
would never mean
       anything
no matter how many you wrote.

There's a taste when you choke
on the inside of your throat,
and you savor the realization
you're just another joke.

So you stop trying to breathe
and you just leave your hope
in the inner-lacings
of the noose of that rope –

      and you let go

SMOKERS COUGH

It started at sixteen, when she had her first puff,
it became a habit, until that wasn't enough.
She began going through 3 packs a day,
not knowing the price she would eventually pay.
She inhaled deep and long, blackening her lungs,
wreaking of a stench that covered her tongue.
Made it to twenty one, we all were surprised
but you could tell she was corroded inside.
Such a beautiful girl, with a smokers cough;
announced dead yesterday, on the floor of her loft.

Your love was so shallow
I broke my arms and legs jumping in
I felt there was no real risk
I didn't need to swim
but I just ended up face down,
in a couple inches of your love –
        and drowned in it.

"Just tell me I did the right thing" She said as she bit her quivering lip.

"You did the right thing. You did," Her friend assured her. "He's going to get to live, and so will you. Now nothing is going to get in the way of the future you both want."

Her friend wheeled her out of the front doors of the hospital and helped her into the car. The car ride was quiet and she looked out of the window until the front of her house came into view.

"Thanks" She said as she got out of the car quickly, avoiding any further communication.

Years had passed. Her life had flourished in ways she never deemed possible, she experienced happiness she didn't know existed. She checked in on him, sometimes, she saw his life mirror hers in many ways and she felt that.. her friend didn't lie to her. She did do the right thing. Though, it didn't stop her from feeling how she felt. It didn't stop her from wanting to have him empathize with her sometimes. She needed to see him and she knew exactly where to find him.

"Duncan" she said, as she called to the back of the head she knew all too well. He turned searching for the voice that called him.

"Dani? Wow, how are you?" He reached out to hug her, "It's been like what, two years?"

"Three. I'm good, though. How 'bout you?"

"Good, good.. wow, crazy. You look so different." He looked her up and down "What are you doing in my neck of the woods?"

"Neck of the woods?"

"Sorry.. that's kind of nothing I would say unless I were saying it ironically" He smiled, "Do you maybe want to go for a drink or something later and catch up? I gotta finish up here but I will be free around 8?"

"Sure, I'll meet you here." She turned and disappeared down the street as Duncan's eyes followed her and a faint grin crossed his face.

As she looked in the mirror and applied her eyeliner she thought about the night to come. She rehearsed to herself what she was going to say to him. She rehearsed until it was just right. She straightened out her blouse and smoothed out any last wrinkles. Before knocking on the door she took a deep breath, realizing that perhaps she wasn't as prepared as she had anticipated. The door swung open.

"Hey, Dani. Good timing" He said as he locked up behind him, "Does it matter where we go?"

"Nope, I'm cool with wherever"

He lead her down the busy downtown streets parting through pre-drunk crowds of the locals. Each busy bar they passed she wondered where he was going to take her. He grabbed her hand and they turned a corner and walked into a nightclub that hadn't yet gotten the crowd for the night. He nodded his head to a bouncer and reached over the bar, grabbing a 26oz of vodka and two glasses between his fingers.

They ended up at the back end of the club in a booth where she imagined the important people would be seated. It seemed that was him now. She sat down and watched him as he poured out a drink for her. He smiled and the black light made his teeth glow neon blue, she giggled to herself.

In attempt to ease her nerves she threw back her drinks at record speed, not really accounting for how unintelligible she might be as she drops a bomb on him. In no time they were laughing, joking and fooling around like old times, she had missed him. He watched as her eyes became low and a little glossy and her posture had relaxed. He felt good knowing that she was getting comfortable with him again. His eyes watched as she spoke and licked her lips at every pause and he felt an urge growing inside of him that he couldn't control. As her hand skimmed his arm he dove into her lips attempting to linger long enough that he could close the gap of three absent years much quicker.

"You.." she touched her lip "kissed me"

"Yeah" he swallowed hard

"Look, I have to tell you the real reason I'm here..."

"So it wasn't because you missed me, or something?"

"I did, I do..." She paused, trying to find the words, "I don't know if I should say anything and up until right now I still had second thoughts. I don't want to ruin your life. I—"

"Ruin my life?"

"Yeah"

"What could you tell me that would ruin my life?" He looked confused, "Is it my mom, is she okay? Did something happen to her?"

"No, it's—she's fine. It's not about your mom okay.. it's about us."

"What about us?"

She felt panic building up inside of her she couldn't say these words to him. A forced smile crept across her face and she pulled him in and kissed him. Alarmed at first, he went wide eyed then eased into the idea quickly and embraced her as they kissed profoundly. Her fingers trailed up his chest and he began to breathe heavily. Neither of them realized the crowd that had begun to gather in the nightclub. No one would have noticed their indiscretions but Duncan decided to relocate anyways. Lips still pressed together he began to stand up pulling her with him and they disappeared up the back stairway that lead to the managers office. They found their way to a small leather sofa and he began pulling off items of their clothing, doing the undressing for the both of them.

Danielle could feel the alcohol burning her chest, and she could hardly keep her balance as duncan tore items of clothing off of her. Once all that remained was her bra Duncan fell back onto the couch and pulled her down onto his lap. His fingers wandered and she could see how turned on he was, and as he raised her hips to push inside, her quiet attempts to stop it were hushed with their heavy breaths. He filled her. He pulled her in and kissed her neck and chest as he reached for the latch of her black lace bra to undo. Danielle began hyperventilating as tears shot out of her eyes. Duncan stopped his thrusts and moved her back slightly to see her face, to see if the sound he heard was in fact correct. As he looked at her she cried harder and broke down in his arms. He slipped out of her and grabbed his coat on the floor and wrapped it around her.

"What's wrong what happened? What did I do, please tell me?" He begged. But her crying didn't stop and her body remained tense in his arms "Is this about what you came here to tell me?"

A pause in her cries told him yes. She sniffled herself into calmness and he held her tightly. He looked at her with concern but also impatience.

"I really feel like shit right now, what's going on, Dani?"

"W-w-when we were t-t-t-together, that n-night" she cried, "At prom"

"What about it, hun? Tell me, you're scaring me"

"I-I got.."

"Pregnant..?"

She cried into his shirt fearing to see his expression of connecting the dots. He would know there was no way she could have a living child for three years and have not known a thing about it.

He gently slipped from her grasp and stood up. He straightened out his jeans and slipped them on and threw on a shirt. The room seemed to start spinning. A blank expression was plastered on his face but an anger built inside of him quietly.

"FUUCK" he screamed as he threw everything on the desk to the floor and kicked and punched at the wall. Tears welled up in his eyes "Fuck fuck fuck. No no no no no"

Danielle watched fighting back her tears. It hurt to see him in so much pain, this is what she feared would happen in telling him. She put her arms in the coat as she cautiously stepped towards him as his head was pressed into the wall and his fists clenched. She touched his sides and slowly put her head to his back. He tensed but didn't respond for a moment until he pulled her arm all the way around his waist before turning around.

"I'm sorry" she said

"I know why you did it."

"You do?"

"We were young. Secondly, that was right when I got my opportunity to go to abroad for basketball. Right?"

"I just didn't want you to miss a chance like that, it's once in a lifetime."

"So are kids, for some people"

"I wanted you to live your life, become an adult in our dump of a city who actually has their shit together. I'm sorry I decided without you, I'm sorry I told you now. But I wanted to make you a happier man."

"*You* made me happy, Danielle! Do you know how hard it was to leave you behind?"

"Yeah, so hard you never came back."

"Exactly. It was so hard I never came back. I didn't want to come home to you to have you turn me away, I couldn't lose you and walk away from you twice."

"You know I would have taken you back."

"Maybe that's the other part of it, maybe part of me knew you'd take me back and I felt I didn't deserve that. Didn't deserve a second chance after choosing basketball over you."

"I wanted you to go. You worked so hard for it. I didn't want to take that away from you over some mistake."

"You think you getting pregnant was an accident?" He looked at her almost in disgust "God wanted it. We used protection. God wanted that for us. And you know what? *I* wanted that for us. I would have taken a son or daughter with you over a basketball career any day. But, it doesn't matter, I'm not even mad at you."

"You seem mad"

"I'm not. I know that in the fucked up shit you do your intentions are good and your heart is in the right place. I also know I wasn't easy to go to back then. I know that I might have been a coward then. This reaction you're getting may not have been what you got at that time. So I just want to know one thing.. one thing that will make this all worth it..."

"What?"

"Are you happy?"

"I am now."

"Do it"

He pushed.

"I can't"

"Do it!!" He hollered.

"No, I'm not. I- I- I can't." She cried

"You have to" He said sternly as he clasped her finger on the trigger and pushed the cold metal to his sweaty forehead. He knew what needed to happen and no matter how much he insisted she did it, he feared the pain she would feel "Please"

It was like she wasn't even there. She was beside herself. She looked at him beg and for a moment she wondered how she could even do this. He was her brother. Then she saw his open flesh ripped by the jaws of a monster. Her brothers eyes were already being clouded by crimson veins and his sockets were sinking in. The longer she delayed his death the angrier at her he seemed to be getting.

Still in a daze she held the gun at his head. He went to say something but all that escaped was a growl. She cried and scoffed as she breathed heavily and steadied her stance even though the gun was at his head and she couldn't miss. She winced until she shut her eyes tightly and pulled the trigger.

She weakly whimpered and swallowed hard and she choked up a tearless cry. She fell back on the grass next to him, with the gun still tightly clutched in her hand. She felt empty and couldn't feel her limbs. As she stared up at the night sky that still seemed to have millions of stars, she felt angry. Like as though the universe were mocking her.

We're alive and shining bright, and down there; *you're all undead.*

I first tore my skin
with a blade
when it seemed
like
the fact I felt
as though
I didn't matter,
didn't matter.

And I only stopped,
because I ran out
of pure skin to scathe.

92 POUNDS

Though the scale
said a number that'd suffice,
blood drained from her face
her skin cold as ice

Her eyes dull green,
a meshed hue of dead trees
she looked at her reflection,
no way to describe what she sees

That was when it hit her,
the reason she could only frown..
it was – she loved herself so little;
she could only love 92 pounds.

NEWS

Sanity escapes me
sometime during the news
people do things
that leave me confused.
There are monsters
who wake up and choose:

'I'm going to fuck this world up,
over some brand new shoes,
a grudge, some booze,
or for a midnight cruise,'

Like, what is your muse?
Did no one love you?
How could you be amused,
by all this abuse
inflicted on innocent people,
whose life could ensue
a better world,
better values and virtues?
What's your excuse –
             When we all lose?

UP IN FLAMES

I didn't die in that fire.
I guess you are surprised.
You thought that I was weak,
that I would burn beneath your lies.

You forgot one thing about me,
and it's that I don't give in.
You had wished that I would fail,
so I made sure that I would win.

So this is for the fire,
you lit because of me.
Here is the lighter,
and here's the gasoline.

I've turned up the music
and I've turned up the TV
I hope you burn in hell,
no one will hear your screams

I'm the one who did it,
don't forget my name.
I'm the one who set
the Devil up in flames.

PERCEPTION

I cry sometimes
at what people think
about me
who I am,
what I do,
about how I must feel to,
be:

"So quiet and focused
determined and refined,
beautiful and elegant –
graceful and talented,
wise beyond your years,
mysterious and simple –
            alive"
Well I wonder,
if they ever realize sometimes
that what they think
            is wrong.

I WAS ELEVEN

I was 11 when I nearly lost my life.
My friends and I were playing outside with handcuffs from the
joke shop.
I had my hands cuffed behind my back and was trying to get free –
when I fell.

It rained the previous night
and I happened to fall face first into a puddle
I tried to shuffle and turn my head once I realized I couldn't
breathe;

A part of me refused to show my struggle
I wanted to get out of this by myself.

It scared me, because that was the day
I realized
I would rather die
(In three inches of dirty water no-less)

than ask for help.

By day

Every sip of red wine reminded my lips of your tongue that night
and how I felt your intrigue as you parted my knees to slink in
between

At the time,
I felt thuds deep in my chest fifty times what it should beat

And now it seemed as sobriety seeped in, our minds weren't
clouded with poor judgement, just reality, knock,

knock,

knocking demanding to be realized. Demanding to remind you
that there is guilt in your pleasures if you had to keep them a
secret.

Or why else is something that feels so good, something you need to
hide?

I wish you loved me in public.

I can't really write,
when I've got this much on my mind
I can't write when I'm trying
to act like everything's fine.

I can't write,
when it's all bottled up in me,
I can't say what I want,
while I'm so unhappy.

I can't write at all,
I don't even want to sleep,
I woke up today,
hoping yesterday was a dream.

I can't really write,
because when it's all done and said,
this will just be a poem,
and you will still be dead.

ANYMORE

You don't own me anymore,
I found this out today.
your actions don't haunt my dreams,
and your face has faded away

You're not my monster
you're not here, and I do not fear
you couldn't hold on to my soul,
the words you said, I no longer hear.

I lost a few years, trying
crying, simply simplifying..
why you did it to me, but
when I realized, I'm not dying

I just didn't give a fuck, why.
I just thought about who.
A few years, to discover, it matters
not why, but who you give your heart to.

Such a precious treasure,
so never wear it on your sleeve.
enclose within such brittle bones,
but it still belongs to me.

ESCAPISM

Your lips tasted like gin and I was love drunk. I swam in your intoxication and we floated along one another's skin. I couldn't figure out why with a sober mind I couldn't find the nerve to speak to you, nor you the nerve to speak to me. But it seemed that on our alcohol consumed weekends we found each other even on the dimmest nights.

We spoke as if we had been best friends for centuries, as if we had been in love for years. Although the only times we could say anything worth hearing to each other we were in this haze. But a drunken tongue is an honest one –

And by day our sober minds don't remember how good it was

I DRINK

I drink..

Maybe a little too often
and maybe a little too much,
but

I can stop.
If I wanted to,
but I like to drink.

I drink to celebrate!
and to mourn..

I'm just torn
I don't know
whether I drink
to remember
or to forget
        anymore.

DESTRUCTIVE

"I'm very comfortable in my destruction."

"What? What do you mean?"

"I mean. I'm very comfortable being here with you." She inhaled her cigarette as she buttoned up her blouse, "Comfortable fucking you, when I know it's wrong."

He looked at her perplexed. She turned the key in the ignition and started the car as she smirked proudly. He didn't take his eyes off of her the entire car ride. He studied her, trying to figure her out, but to no avail. She was a closed book, even when she smiled – was it joy, sadness? He wasn't even sure she knew. They pulled up to his house and he snapped out of his squandering.

"We're here" She flicked her cigarette out of the car window, "Say hi to your wife for me."

She joked comfortably. She smiled in satisfaction but she was not yet done destructing the night.

RUNAWAY

I know you think I ran away
but its becoming kind of hard to say,
why I left my house,
why I packed my bags,
why I left people I've known for half my life without a word to say.
Why I liked leaving my past behind,
escaping to places they couldn't find me.

I don't know why home isn't home,
or why home is when I'm alone

THEY SAY THE DRUG CHANGES YOU

I didn't really think too much of it, but it's true. I give up on everyone. I don't even know if I'll be able to love anyone long enough to be in a relationship. My standards are so ridiculously out of reach, that not even a rocket could reach them. It made me think I deserved whatever star in the sky I desired, if not all of them. I've been empty, cold, apathetic. I've found comfort in corruption. I've found sanity in the destruction of myself. Every piece of me that broke, felt like what was meant to happen. I chant powerful positive praise, but I don't know what I really believe. I don't know who I really am.. I'm different now.. And the scariest part is knowing I can't turn back. They say the drug changes you, I didn't really think much of it, but it's true.

WHICHEVER ROAD YOU CHOOSE TO TRAVEL

I'm in love with talent,
and I'm in love with you
In love with your mind
and what you aspire to do

I'm in love with a furrowed brow,
and an expression not confused
but the face of an artist
deep in the zone; in tune
– with what they choose

In love with the blues –
in love with a rush
a changeable view
In love with creations fighting
to escape and are long overdue

In love with the message
hidden beneath strokes, strums and hues
In love with the existential search;
of not where I belong
– but rather which me I belong to.

GRENOBLE

I've walked home alone many dark mornings
where the air was cold, the grass was wet
and you could hear nothing but a distant car
every 340 steps or so. I've spent miles
walking, wanting to understand if I'd ever
reach a destination that felt right, rather
than one that was just familiar. I never really
had to think twice to end up here,
I never had to overlook my shoulder fearing
I'd be followed. I was safe, except from myself.
It was only after walking, who knows where,
during a dark morning where the air was crisp,
there was no grass and only bike bells and footsteps
crossed paths with me. I spent a night
lying on the pavement outside of a train terminal,
trying to cling to the sleep I'd been desperately
craving since 6am that morning, but a skepticism
kept me opening one eye every seven and a half minutes
to see if I was still alive or floating in the last
moments of my life. I wasn't safe, not even from myself.
But it was a serene feeling to experience
who I was, when I was walking
somewhere other than, home
alone.

Don't drink me

I hunched over the toilet spilling over what was left of my lunch, it continued until the acids burned my throat and I had nothing left to purge. I stood up and rinsed my face. My reflection was no longer familiar to me. The music blasting through the other side of the door shook the mirror and I felt the room begin to spin and I toppled onto the floor.

I let my eyes fall shut with only the ceiling light in my view. The room spun faster as my eyes were closed but I had lost control. I'm disgusting. All I could think of as I laid there was what a mess I've become. Drinking away my problems only to realize I create more when I'm intoxicated. Only to realize, my problems don't go away. They hide.

They hide until they leach onto my skin and become one with me. They suck and suck the life out of me, the purpose, until I am the problem. Infecting everyone else. I am poison.

I'M NOT BEAUTIFUL WHEN I WRITE

I can't count how many times
I've hysterically tapped at my keyboard
trying to get out words
that my throat tightened around,
trying to act un-phased
as my tears dripped
through each illuminated
space between the keys
but clearly,
I had cried too many,
it grew an immunity
to my hurt

I don't quaintly sip tea,
or other caffeine,
as I'm struck by a beautiful idea

I spend my late drunken nights,
my mascara further
blackening the bags of my eyes
only further upsetting me,
"Wow, I still need makeup to feel beautiful"

I'll cry harder;
feeling I've failed as a human being.

I'll continue to write
about all sorts of things
that to my family,
I'd deny were true,

Like,
that girl I once wrote about
with the eating disorder
or the one who
cuts her skin
to see if she can still
feel anything..

Well, I come back to these keys
like it's a disease
because with a protruding ribcage
and cuts across the street
of my arms –
I'll fall apart.

Because I will never know,
how to be beautiful when I write..

I can only write things
that I wish I could be
I even write characters
with small glimpses,
or are me to a tee
you gaze at them beautifully
so it's confusing, you see..

Why is my writing,
more beautiful than me?

ESCAPE

I drank until drinking didn't make me drunk. I got high until it took a life time supply to get me there. Though, no matter my choice of escaping I always seemed to be at rock bottom. The worst part about trying to escape with substances is; it's an illusion. It's not a tax write off, it's not a diploma, it's not a home, it's not a lover, it just makes you forget temporarily you have none of these things. Until your hunger, your thirst for the illusion becomes another dream you can't have and can't achieve. Until you starve not only literally, but mentally for the ability to even imagine yourself if you had not been such an utter waste. *But you can't, can you?* This realization is when no two-six, no spliff, no pills, not even the hardest drugs can help you escape this time. Just, cold heavy metal. As it penetrates your mouth, you close your eyes – hoping it be quick and kind. And as your lips kiss the stainless steel you can just taste your escape.

TRAVELA

My judgments are not influenced by love
I've lived in the unrequited area of it too long
my passion lies in new city ties,
and in countries, I don't belong

I'm not running from my life,
I'm not even running away from home
I'm just inching towards the chance,
to matter on my own

My bags are packed with not a lot
there's not much I'd want to bring
just my dream and the means
to make the best of things

I'll feel at home no matter where,
whenever I look up to the sun
no matter how far you are from home,
it's always the same one

So don't worry if you lose me,
as I'm across the map in my travels
because the purpose in the end
of this journey will be unraveled.

DEATH OF ME

I've been so painfully forcing myself
to fit in the confined space of conformity
camouflage my beliefs of societies expectations
that mold me so forcefully.
I am society, I've cut, purged and
bludgeoned the real me outside of me.
I've lost sight and I worship fake trivial
contradictions that don't apply to me.

I drowned myself in the undermined voices
once screaming to be heard
I've suffocated her genius, her obliqueness,
the whole uniqueness of her.
She's cried and I lie as I've tried to proceed
to punish and silence her worth.
I beat her inches from her life,
I was going to erase her from earth.

But she screamed so solidly
I felt my entire body freeze
She shook from inside of me,
angrily, somehow putting me at ease.
'You were born to stand out,' She began,
'Why can't that be?'
I realized, molding myself to societies perfection –
will be the death of me.

STRING

I like to string words together. Just like that sentence, perhaps. I love to dance with words and make them paint an elegant picture that flows like a ballet dancer on her toes. I love my words to be the dialogue of a visionary. I want to sketch a comic from scene to scene that leads you to a climax. I want to somehow creatively embed the yarn of my mind into yours. I sometimes hope that I can breaststroke through your thoughts allowing my words to vicariously tread through you. I want to echo in your mind in the most absolute silence, when you feel you have gone deaf. I want to tip toe in the back of your mind that you neglect because it sometimes hurts. I want to parade through your beliefs as my words encourage you to stand up for them. I want to lovingly lie in your heart as you feel my words describe your infatuation. Connection is such a beautiful thing, and I want to connect you to my words that I attach with some string.

12 MONTHS AGO

"There are days like this where I cry through my laughs." I shrugged as I wiped a tear from the bags under my eyes, "I'm just exhausted you know, and it's hard moving past things sometimes and—"

I felt my throat tighten and my words made me choke, so I stopped myself. My sister embraced me as she felt me crumble in her arms. She rambled the usual, things will get better and everything happens for a reason. I just nodded agreeably because I knew she was trying her best to comfort me. Though, nothing was comforting about a feeling like this.

"Hey.." My neighbor walked towards us while we sat on my doorstep, "How you doin' kiddo?"

"Fine" I forced myself to say.

"I'll let you two talk" My sister stood up, "Are you hungry, though? I can make something"

"No. I'm okay. Thanks" My sister nodded and stepped inside.

"I didn't know you had another sister up until a few days ago.. When I met her at the hospital" He said in hopes for an explanation.

"She's my half sister, we share the same mom" I looked around uninterested in our conversation. He could tell because he changed it pretty quickly as he examined me for a new topic.

"Have you.. um… been taking your medication?"

"Uh huh" I answered snobbishly

"I'm just asking because I care.. and because your bandage is leaking through.. so you've obviously not been taking the blood thickener pills."

I looked down at the crimson red spill seeping through the bandage around my wrists. I've been drinking excessively for eleven months so my blood never seems to stop pouring out of me. I stood up and ran inside. I shut the door quickly behind me and took a deep breath.

I heard my sister call me from the kitchen but I ignored her to rush to the bathroom. I unraveled the bandage drenched in my blood and dumped it into the trash.

My cuts hurt, all 12 of them. One for each month since my dad died. The twelfth one put me in the hospital last week. I think my friends, and everyone knew that I cut myself.. but I wonder if they knew that everyday, I cut each gash until the month was done.

My thoughts were disrupted by a faint knock on the door. And I watched the rest of my blood disappear into the drain.

"Hun? Here. I have your bandage" My neighbor turned the locked nob.

I looked around realizing I hadn't brought the bandages up with me and opened the door to his concerned face. He nudged his head for me to sit, and I hiked myself on the counter. He ran a wet cloth over my cuts cleaning off the remaining blood. He clenched his jaw as he tore off a piece of gauze and placed it on my mutilated wrists, supporting my hands so gently and wrapped them with care. He looked up at me as he sealed the closure together and I bit the inside of my lip and looked away.

"They look a lot worse. Have you done anything to them today?"
"No. The last time was 8 days ago. I'm fine."

"You know, you keep saying that shit, but then you get admitted into the emergency room" He saw the look on my face go blank. And he grabbed my face to get me to focus on him, "I'm so worried about you, this is why I bother you and check up on you and call you every five minutes. You scare me so much, and I don't want to lose you"

He kissed my forehead and then squeezed my head to him as I cried on his chest. "I love you okay?" I nodded within his grasp, he repeated, "Okay?!"

"Okay."

WHEN YOUR HEART IS OVERSEAS

When your heart is across the oceans
and it's continents away
when your heart is anywhere but here
and there are no other words to say but,
it's yours – do you want it?
When your eyes open each morning
to a ceiling you pray is there or theirs or anywhere.
When you crave that the breeze brushing your scalp
were their fingers through your hair.
When your passion is in altitudes higher than the birds
or deep in tides where land is just a word,
of a thing, that you have never seen.
A word that must embody something
you have only dreamed,
like how you dream of your love across the globe.
When all you've ever wanted and all you've ever known
was never how to stay but only how to go.

How do you deal, when your heart is overseas
wherever you may be?

EXISTENTIALISM

SHE

I write 'she' instead of me. Instead of I. I find it easier to say, she wants to die. I find it easier to express how badly I'm hurt through someone else's life that seems has some worth. See if I tell you that she's beautiful, that's the image you'll be forced to see. But if I say I'm beautiful you'll be stuck envisioning me.

So I share my stories through a girl I've never seen. A girl that in many ways I have never been. I've described myself with a smile that I have never gleamed. With a purpose, with a wit, with morality, with a substance, more anything, than I have ever dreamed.

So I do write myself as me hypothetically except she is honest. Is pure. She's not sure of everything but she makes the best out of a bad situation. She is curious. Passionate. Intriguing. Delicate. She is mixed up, but very simplistic which she feels very few people will ever discover. She is more than her exterior.

She is misunderstood, sometimes genius, loving, but scared so she keeps her distance. For instance. Her first love lived approximately twenty-two hundred and six miles away. For millions of people they would be physically and emotionally starved, but in fact. She was most comfortable like that. She wants to be held but doesn't want to ask. She wants to act on how she feels without moving too fast.

She wants to please everyone, but she can't so herself. So she puts on a mask and pretends to be strong, tries to blend in to seem like she belongs. But the truth of it all is that she will never blend in, she will never follow the pack, she will never be happy like that.

She isn't hopeless, but she's still a stupid little girl sometimes who demands respect she shouldn't get. She just requires something genuine because she has a void to fill.

See, she can admit that, but I never will.

I CAN'T LET YOU LOVE ME

I can't let you love me
I can't let your
inner flame,
your internal passion,
be doused by
this self-pitying, insecure,
worthless, ungrateful,
stupid teenage girl

Over your sneaking suspicion,
that I *might* be worth it.

The people you love and the ones who love you will show you who you really are. They will show you what you like, what you hate, what you can't stand, what will make you violent, what will show you a side of you that no one, not even you; knew existed.

You will be taught lessons that you will have to relearn almost every day. They will show you how strong you are capable of being and in many ways – how weak.

They will uncover your flaws, and if they love you, they will admire them. If they don't, there is someone else for you. They will sometimes make you feel undeserving of their love, or maybe they are undeserving of yours.

They will be your everything and nothing. But the thing most important about the people you love and the ones who love you is; they will show you who you really are.

WHY I THINK PEOPLE FALL IN LOVE WITH ME

I make my complexities, simple. I make all the reasons I can't love you, can't stand you, can't share you – make sense. In showing me, I show you who you are. I show you what you're capable of overcoming. I uncover your strength, in showing you mine.

I strip down my insecurities so you can see them, so you have the chance to run from them. I give you an out. In me setting you free, you crave for me to care more. In me being okay with showing my flaws, you realize the effort you need to put in to be okay with yours. You want to not give a fuck like I don't, but you do.

I've only ever needed myself, and that bothers you. It bothers you but you respect it and you admire it, but when you want to be with me – you want me to need you. If I don't need you, you serve no purpose. If I don't need you, you need to be something extra; something I don't already have.

I am distant. Even when you kiss me and hold me you can tell my heart is miles away. You didn't care about my heart before but now that you can't have it – it's all you can think about. You've fallen into a blur. You're not sure when or why you cared so much about being the one I love, but you do; and you hate that you're not.

When I breathe, in moments that should take my breath away. When I smile, in moments that I should drown in heart wrenching tears. When I can still think, in skull crushing moments. When I am everything you are not, I think that – that is when people fall in love with me.

I guess I just wonder, when they will discover that really; they're falling in love with a girl who use to care too much, who is insecure but would rather you see now, than leave later, a girl who had her heart broken, who had been hurt physically, emotionally, and now suffers psychologically.

I am a prisoner of my own mind. If you would have known better, you'd know you should not fall for my kind.

I don't want to be like her

I don't want to be like her,
So I hate it when I am.
I fake our connection
and avoid it when I can.

I don't want to be a coward,
the way she cowers to her man.
I don't want to think,
that's the best I can demand.

I don't want to be trapped,
beneath belittling words.
I don't want to be treated,
the way he mistreats her.

I don't want to be like her,
and doubt who I can be.
I love myself far too much,
to be anyone but me.

PAINT

She was an artist;
that much was true,
she made an ocean
with 6 different hues.
Once she said she used
34 shades of green,
thirty-four shades,
to paint a forest
she had seen,
but once.

She saw things in a way
no non-artist
could ever see
she lived in the art,
she thought
she'd never be.

A thousand words,
did not sum up her work,
they hardly put a dent
but out there'd be a writer,
who'd use every
hour spent trying
defying her
ridiculously high
standard of art

With his linguistics
and familiarity with
characteristics,
that come along with
a work of art,
that carry the artists heart
through each jagged stroke
and fainted shade
not that anyone
paid attention

This writer would know
there was more
to the colours she chose
and how they were
chronologically placed
and how each face,
reminded her of
someone.

The writer would taste
each pause in her pace,
each linger
each finger
that she embraced
the brush with.
They'd love how
she smelled like paint
even though it was faint
it'd be the smell
they thought of all day.

And she'd know
and they'd know,
you're the best thing I've painted,
you're the best thing I've written –
to date.

I DON'T LIKE FLOWERS

I don't like flowers, but
there's something ironic about that;
I resemble them in volumes
Losing petals off my back
after I've bloomed
and the rises and falls of the moon
have passed many fortnights
and sometimes people pass me just as those daisies,
like they are too lazy to stop and smell the roses,
occasionally I just wish someone would pick me
and let me live with my feet off the ground
even if for only a few moments
before I die in their arms
I'm the tulips of first loves
and the nights they get dreamed of
I don't like flowers, but
begonias, lotus', calla lilies;
are a little bit like me.

It's funny

How I feel so empty,
but I fill pages with words.
How I love so deeply,
with a heart that just hurts.

How I smile so big,
and even fester a laugh.
How I guide others,
while unsure of *my* path.

How I hold you,
without crying.
Carry you,
without trying.

I do all you need of me,
without dying –

and it's just funny.

Hippy

I want to be a hippy,
a fun-loving free spirit
with an inability to worry
I want to take risks
without needing a safety net
I want to speak before I think
because I don't want
to care anymore
about offending others
with my opinions

I want to be a hippy
I want to enjoy each moment
and connect with others
simply because of an aura
that makes me genuinely believe
this is a person with ideas
and dreams
and wants to see the worlds growth

I want to be a hippy—
full figured woman
loving every curve I was blessed with
realizing;
there's just more of me to love

I want to be a hippy
awakened and embracing the truth
I want to stop keeping time
and just explore until I'm through

YOU HAVE NOT LOVED ME

You have not loved me until you have been buried alive beneath cold and suffocating expectations. You have not loved me until you have understood how it feels to always be wrong. You have not loved me if you still love bravely. You *have* loved me if you understand loss and sacrifice. You have loved me if I was the best and worst thing in your life. You have loved me if you're delicate. But, if you're not – you have not loved me.

IF I HAD A SAY

I'd have chosen
to be a genderless-being
without a race
without human manipulation
causing me to think a certain way

I'd have chosen to discover things
the way humans use to
before the internet and electricity
and all the innocence
the media robs us of

I'd have experienced life
not knowing the dangers
only wonders
experiencing a racing pulse,
dizziness, laughter
tears — confusion
but being so engaged
and in tune with who I am;
whatever that implies

If I had a say,
I'd unlearn all that makes me judgmental,
guarded, boring and too scared
to live a life that'd be
sporadic, thrilling
and completely fulfilling

I LIKE WHEN YOU CRY

I like when you cry. It reminds me that you're human. That you have feelings. But most importantly, it reminds me that you can care about something. How do you brush things off so easily? I wonder why you can get completely disrespected, humiliated, betrayed and near death and still.. function. Smiling in peoples faces like you have the perfect life. I watched you for forever being so damn... positive. Finding the bright side in everything, fucking shining your sunlight on everyone and puking up fucking rainbows and lollipops. You went through so much bullshit and you still smile. But sometimes.. the worst of times, when everything catches up to you and everyone else is gone, you look me in the eye and I see your lip quiver. I see the way you cringe at how your heart aches. I see the tears building up and then.. we cry together. I'm your reflection and I'm the only one you cry in front of. I like when you do. It reminds me that you're real. Even if I'm not. I am just reflective glass coated with metal amalgam; wondering how it feels to cry.

TIDES

I miss floating;
just resting inches
beneath the surface
looking up
appreciating how little I felt
in a body of water
and beneath a sky
bigger than my dreams

All I know now
is sinking feet deep
beneath a surface
fearing how little I feel
just a body in water
with only the memory of a sky
and getting far too deep
to breathe

and being swallowed whole
by the sea

I'm like the moon
    on the nights
it refuses to show
    it's whole self.

HUMANS

I think it was too much to expect, that complex machines like us, would function correctly. There is so much wrong with all of us, I'm amazed we have not all collapsed. Why has my mind not exploded trying to understand itself? I don't know, but it's too much to expect, for me to be able to deal with what has come of my undeniable cranial wanderings. I'm going insane, and I can feel it. I'll have certain moments where I can feel myself corroding from the inside out. I can feel my heart turn to charcoal, and crumble along with my skin. My emotional scars are becoming real and turn to magma while eroding through my veins, rendering hurt as the norm. The crimson blood is confusing me with the color of my essence, as I've seen it every time I look at myself. I'm trying to bandage my wounds to incognito. Though they are gashes much too deep to hide behind a thin gauze and they refuse to stop bleeding. Humans are remarkable you see, but they are silly to believe that they are a properly functioning machine.

WHAT, NOT WHOM

If there is anything worse than knowing you have a disorder, it is not. Not knowing but wishing that you do because you want to have an excuse for the insanity that is your brain. It's not knowing why you get mad when someone buys you gifts. Not knowing why you hate people saying they love you. Not knowing why seeing your nephew mixing multiple colors of playdoh together makes you slightly ill. Not knowing why things not going as planned makes you feel like you burn from the inside out. Not knowing why you need to be perfect but fall in love with imperfect people. Not knowing why when you're angry you have the desire to rip off faces. Not knowing why when you get corrected you turn into a raging bitch. Not knowing why you don't like cuddling and feed off of personal space. Why you hate being affectionate more than an hour a day. Why you feel sad after you laugh. Why you can't cry actual tears sometimes, even though you crinkle your nose and feel a mental break down coming on. Why you run away every time someone wants you longer than just a day. Why you turn away compliments even though you sometimes believe they are true. Why you need the kitchen light on while you're in the family room, why you notice when it goes off. Why you need to fall asleep to sound. Why you find comfort in watching shows you're 'too old' for. Why you dream about the things stressing you out and wake up every ten minutes because you're actively worrying about if the day to come is going to blow up in your face. Why sleeping is hard. Why waking up is harder. Why you've stopped wondering who you are, and rather – just what.

"I DIDN'T WANT TO LIVE ANYMORE"

She said as she looked up with wide eyes, "But then I heard your voice and I felt.. a warmth cover my skin like a blanket. You didn't tell me to smile. Like everyone use to, thinking it was just that easy. You said–"

"Do you want to talk about it over coffee?" He finished.

She faintly nodded, "I don't know why, but those were the right words. Not even because I find comfort in coffee, you couldn't have known, but it was right. That day basically told me.. someone cares. Someone always does."

He looked at her only now realizing the impact he had, had on her. He felt himself crumble inside. She was satisfied with so little. He was perfectly capable of giving her more, but he hadn't. He hadn't because she had never asked, he hadn't because she was always content with what he had given her. But it was only now that he could put together that it was because – she had less than nothing more often than not.

I hear you're in love
        I'm sorry

I FALL IN LOVE WITH POSSIBILITY, THAT'S MY GIFT AND MY FUCKING PROBLEM

I fall in love with possibility, that's my gift and fucking problem. The minute I meet you I think of all the things we can accomplish together. If you're an artist all I think is, we can mix colors, techniques, patterns, pain and my strain that being a perfectionist has on my creativity in my art. And my fear to color outside the lines. But I'm dreaming that you can show me how.

If you're a writer I feel that we can expand on more than just vocabularies but expand in which ways our words can touch others. In which ways our stories can be as real to our readers as they were to us as we crawled through them and barely made it out alive.

If you're an athlete I want you to explore my competitive side that also teaches me a loss is part of the process of getting better. I want you to challenge me and forget that I am a girl, forget that you're interested. Treat me like a real competitor so I know you are who are, always.

And, if you're just a man who I spotted and had the smallest connection with. I apologize in advance for picturing what our kids would be like, and the story I'd tell them of how you proposed — assuming we could get that far without my habit; of ending a relationship with the fear I'd mess it up anyway, intervening.

And if you're a woman, I want you to know I think about the possibility with us too. I think of your beauty and how I don't even care that on the street it'll be you that other men or women check out. I think about holding your hand and letting you see the side of me that men wouldn't get and I don't normally show. I think of the things only another woman could understand and how that would make my love for you flow deeper than the wetness between your inner thighs; behind the damn that only I know how to break the way that it does when we are together. I think of it, I think of it often. But also, I apologize to you because I too have become fluent in the possibility that I won't be brave enough to be who I am in public.

But, I am in love with possibility, it's my gift
and possibly one day it won't be a fucking problem.

LONE LIONESS

My loneliness
has just become
that friend who
almost always
pushes me to the edge,
who
almost always
makes me lose it,
who
almost always
makes me want to
disappear..

but I'll come back,
because after all
true friends are rare,

and I need you,
to become more familiar
with myself.

SCARLET

I've always had this bizarre
unfinished scar on my wrist,
like I wanted to cut,
but refrained or resist.
Like something eased me,
and put me in bliss.
Like the thought of the day,
when my love and I kissed.
I gripped the blade tightly,
to be sure not to miss,
when I then felt a change,
and that's when it switched

I was happy for once,
and you were the twist.
You are the beauty in the scar
that's engraved in my wrist.

Undress me

One day
I will take it all off,
I promise
I will strip down to nothing
you can see me
as I am
the bare
naked
truth.
I will watch you
examine each flaw
of my skin
and I guess,
I'll just have to hope
you fall in love with them.

Because when I am naked
and waiting and hoping,
for your approval
and more so,
your admiration

I'll be holding my breath,
not wanting
to fall to pieces
because if I die
right now
starved for air
due to the embarrassment
of not being
pretty enough

I'd at least like to go,
with my eye liner winged,
my concealer
and foundation
evenly distributed,
my lashes elongated
by mascara,
my cheeks dusty rose;
lilac shadows above my eye

and a matte chap
dressed along my lips,
that couldn't hold on
to another breath.

Because,
if you can't love me
undressed ..
Why would that change –
      in death?

I was always told
to treasure the moments
that I was given,
but I have learned
and unlearned
many times.

QUIET

Nights like this;
It's so quiet
my breath
sounds loud
The clock ticks,
my hearts thud
is an actual noise
I hear the shuffle
of me
extending my legs
beneath my sheets..

I freeze.

My ears turn back
to the sound of my heart,
my 'purpose'
It's in unison with the clock,
that's ticks
begin to pluck my nerves
My breathing is too
heavy now,
so I try to stop
completely.

I find,
in the quiet
is the loudest
it could be.

CLICK

One day, I'm hoping it'll just click
in the heat of a moment, when I'm tumbling to rock bottom
in a hurry; like it's going out of style
I hope whatever it is that yanks me down like an anchor
finally opens my eyes, smacks me down to size
and pulls my head out of the clouds,
I hope I can say it aloud, *I hear you.*
I'm ready, this is it.

I hope it just clicks, goes off like a gun
hits like a whip and sends me running to,
sends me running to, rather than from
to a place I felt I've never belonged, as I leave
the one that held me for too long

If it clicks and it fits me
like a glass shoe on the foot of a fairytale-one-of-a-kind chick
If it fits, like my hand in yours, or my head
on your shoulder once did
If it clicks like each step I took down every hallway
I pictured as a red carpet
If it clicks like the flick of the lightbulb switch
that finally shone in my head during 10th grade science
If in my utmost defiance I finally get it,
then it's time to stop avoiding it —
and let myself just fuck up

Then, maybe it might click

THAT PIECE

You know that piece that you read, and you sit back in your seat after the words seep into your brain and you're completely changed. You forgot your name. The characters words are still engraved in your flesh and for a moment you think of whats right, not what you don't have left anymore. Their words made you soar and sore and that was beautiful because you didn't think you felt anymore, not like this. Not hearing words that kiss you on the lips and the crevice of your mind, that makes you rewind time and replay it again so slowly it's like it's standing still. If truth could kill, the words of that piece would torture you 'til death was kind enough to put you out of your misery. It's that piece that weakens you, touches and inspires you and uncovers the desires you truly from the bottom of your heart no matter what your parents say – are very commendable dreams. The piece that makes you revaluate your purpose, whether theres reason to hog all this air that humans share just for someone like you. Someone who isn't always true to who they are and what they do. The piece that makes you feel like you're wasting your life, but also reminds you of a time when you were living it. When you dived in head first and breathed only after three strokes, and when you never choked, you swam in life; breast to back and always deep, you never stopped moving your feet. And, this piece in all it's nostalgia reminds you of how bittersweet the past can be. The kind of piece that makes you want peace of mind, ease and sleep and no more weeping for the day you keep your promise to believe in what you've been breaking your back to achieve. If the dream is still alive this piece is the one that makes you remember it.

I love you more now that it's not my obligation.

YOU READ ME LIKE YOU WROTE ME

As though, my character
was carefully written by you,
in a small cabin,
in the mountains,
where you created art,
from blank pages,
so loud with a hunger,
they craved,
to be engraved in ink

You read me, like
you spent 7 and a half years,
rewriting, remaking, and
recreating, until
it was just the way you wanted –
       layered

With past me's not quite,
gone, as the ink
would bleed through the pages,
but not enough to read,
just enough to wonder:
who could I have been?

You read me,
like an old classic film,
that you can recite,
the entire way through

With the ability,
to capture each moment,
every smile, every sigh,
every millisecond pause,
between the characters,
even the parts where
they get interrupted,
in the middle
of their sentence with
the most corny but passionate –

    Kiss.

You read me, like a kiss,
like you can taste my lips
as my tongue swerves
thoughts that linger onto yours.

The thoughts, I cannot bare
to admit, to you or to me,
the thoughts that, hurt –
the thoughts that are confusing
and don't make a lot of sense
but I just know,
that is the only way to describe it.

You read me as if you wrote me
and, it scares me
            half to death.
If you've written me this far
and we've just now met,
is this the climactic ending?
How many pages, have I got left?

"Are you okay?" He asked.

"With what?" She slowly looked up.

That was just like her to respond in such a way. She saw more than two ways to answer. There were millions and it wouldn't be unusual if she knew every one. She seemed so at peace with how calm she always was but it's really just an overload of her thoughts that numb her completely.

KNOWING YOUR PLACE

Beauty is ranked, and decided by face, by legs, by style and grace. It's defined by the length of your hair, by the amount of guys who stare, and how many people care about you because *you're pretty*.

I think it's shitty that, they forget what's on the inside, that they don't mind brain waves with low tide, as long as you stay fine. Beauty is the deception of quality and misperception of honor and truth, they assume because you are model-Esq that your image of the world is best.

But just like the tides of your mind, your reflection of the world is shallow, untouched and unkind, you don't know much, not even to unravel the outer layers, of peoples skin, to see what's within, is it beautiful still?

Do the thoughts that creep between bleak corners of their mind, and sinful images that arise from time to time, make them beautiful still?

Are the confines of your mind as flawless as your face, or is this a lesson on knowing your place?

My incompetence in love

I feel myself falling hopelessly in love with you. I stare at you, I examine you. The hairs on your arms, the way you furrow your brow, your dimple starts a quarter of a dozen centimeters into your cheek, your lashes are like long blades of auburn grass. You shyly smile when you catch me in admiration, you know I'm in love.

I smile every time you cross my mind, therefore I am never not smiling. It feels so good I fear I'm going to lose it. I battle myself between letting you go before I'm in too deep to risking everything for you. Even my sanity. But little do I know I'm already in too deep; bathing, dissolving in the river that runs through your veins. I can't swim, blood is much thicker than water.

I'll depress myself until I act irrationally.

I'll think I'm not enough, I'll be distant, and when you get mad, I'll assume you were finally realizing I'm not worthy either. Ignoring that maybe, I'm the one who wrung this reaction from you. But I will deny that.

I'm a coward.

So I will ignore the fact that people only leave me because I push them away. I'll ignore the people who have stayed even after I pushed them away. Because, I am so scared to lose someone... that I'll lose myself.

Copies

If you understood how everything
felt like a copy of a copy of a copy —
you'd understand my inability
to feel you the way you're meant to be felt.

You may also get why you're a blur   .
and why your feelings for me are lost in translation

The darkness of this life is no longer jet,
licorice, raven, onyx, charcoal but grey.
Grey, and the worst part of it is,
I'm still trying to figure out what that means.

If I were blue, I would know my mood and how I feel,
But instead everything's a copy of a copy of a copy

        and nothing else is real.

DIG DEEPER

I am deep beneath earth,
millions a' miles south.
Will you search for me?
Even though the air
will get thin?
Even though
the discoveries,
will seem dim?
Even though,
it seems like
you will never
get to the heart,
the root,
of who I really am?
I promise you,
you eventually will
if you keep digging.

Better half

You can have the better half of me,
the one who shall not run scared.
You can have the half of me,
that actually really cares.

You can love her madly
and guaranteed, she'll love you back.
You can live life blissfully,
with my better half.

You can cradle in her grasp,
when she holds you so dear.
You can feel her warmth, and
that her heart beats near.

You can make her replace me,
and you'll be pleased with that.
I'll try not to sulk in my sorrows,
that I'm not my better half.

I want to be comfortable.
I don't want to be
flawless,
perfect,
irreplaceable,
unforgettable,
unique,
if I'm not comfortable.
I don't want to be
pretty,
gorgeous
or thin;

I just want to be comfortable
in my own skin.

How does it feel
to know
I have not lived
since you left?

GREED IS

When you stay with someone you don't deserve. When you kiss them, enjoy them, bask in their company and savor their love. When you hold their hand that has passion carved into their palms. When you allow them to make you into art. When you allow them to put you in their heart and place you on a pedestal so high you develop a fear of heights. When you tell them you love them with everything you have and let them believe it. When you make love to them, fuck them, taste them. When you spend each hour of everyday you can with them when you know you don't deserve it. When you are the happiest and they could be happier. That is greed. But stupidity I guess.. is not taking that opportunity.

Dusk 'til Dawn

The night haunts me through the hollowest of howls
echoes of my past searching for a way out of the shadows
how lonely I feel when they back me against a wall,
paint me into a corner in the narrowest of halls

Their shrieks and screams will never low
and when the grass is cut, the snakes will show
when you leave before the sun does rise
I fear the night will be my demise

Though I've' an empty chest, my heart's not what I miss
I crave for the time I was not too scared to exist
so I'll admit that I'm timid, insecure, silent and scared
but I dread more, the nights that you aren't there

Though if to keep you, I must bring my skeletons to life
I'll let you rest while I battle to survive the night
I'll shut out the voices until they are gone
and I'll wait for you from dusk 'til dawn.

MAYBE IT'S ME

The moment
every failed
     anything
is starting
to crash down
on your
disillusioned
reality
and you begin
to see
maybe
you're not
the problem
     – maybe it's me.

3 REASONS WE'RE FLOWERS

1. We're a planted seed
with all the
potential to grow
and flourish
and —

2. Sometimes we're a dud,
not given the right
circumstances; no love,
attention or light
to survive,
but other times,
we're beautiful
and in our prime,
there's nothing more lovely
than our existence

3. and then, slowly
we start rediscovering
the earth, we feel closer
but we no longer feel
it's sustenance helping us grow
but rather,
laying out a resting place
calling our names,
our souls

until we wilt
and we're back
in the earth
where we
started.

WHERE DO THE STARS GO WHEN IT'S LIGHT OUT

Dim skies and white lies,
chilled wine and blurred lines
act fine, but I can't mean it
haven't hit bottom, but I've seen it
I've been it, caused pain;
driven anyone who has loved me —
insane.

CLOTHING

Her skin draped over her collarbones,
like they were a hanger,
and her flesh was an accessory,
not necessarily to be flaunted
but to be worn religiously,
like the ring her dad gave her
before his permanent home laid beneath
a tombstone

She wore her skin
never in fashion, but in style
her skin was worn,
and so was her smile
she wore her skin through seasons
for reasons more than she could tell,
it itched like wool,
but she wore it well.

Though she fought the flesh,
that dressed her bones
it felt like wearing something,
she didn't own
she feared she would never know,
who she was beneath her clothes.

It was woven on,
she was wearing thin,
could she love what she was in
before it choked her
with embedded threads
or instead,

Will it be,
that she will see

It's not clothing,
hung on her back
it, her skin –
is more than that.

The bridge
of my nose
knows
the pressure
the tips of my fingers
have driven into it
with stressful sighs
with unforgiving cries,
and eye..
haven't let my lips
kiss or utter –
how badly
I miss
my sanity.

BLUES

Have you ever noticed
the color of the morning sky?
It seems like the color
we might see when we cry.
The tint entwined with very vague hues
of China rose and violet too.
The image seen by every heart bruised
is in tune with the sound of the blues.
We're the only ones awake
as early as five,
relating our melancholy
to the shades of the sky.

Out

My thoughts aren't in words,
they're in my glances
In the things I romanticize,
the sighs I let out,
in my desire to stay inside,
in my eyes,
in the simple lies I tell,
to avoid trivial topics
My disgust at gossip,
how I spend my time alone,
how I don't like being on the phone.
They're in how much I drink,
and the nights I've had too much,
in my mood each new years,
and the count down from ten,
in my expression;

My thoughts aren't in words,
they're images corrupting me
from in my mind,
even though I'm out of mine.

WHO YOU ARE

There are parts of me that I wish were parts of someone else. You know, the parts that would make it hard to love anyone. The parts that would make people question how anyone on this earth of some-trillion or so people could ever find you worth their time. Because time is money and although you're a dime; the wealth seems to wither away. All their time, all their energy, all their love is spent endlessly on trying to please you. But you are too hot to the touch and each effort spent burns into flames. You wish that those parts of you would change as you did but they don't. It's like they grow along with the good, because you can't be perfect and those parts – make sure of that. They keep your head out of the clouds but they also put the stars in your eyes. They are lit spheres of imagination that have seen the world in volumes. Those parts are your depth but also your insecurity in being free, they are the bits of you that give you familiarity in being chained to something you see as an impairment. Though, those parts keep your feet firmly planted on the ground – to someone else; those parts are your tell. They are the thing you go silent about, when whoever knows you, knows damn well you love to talk. They are what changes you and has you slip in and out of reality to avoid the side of you, you refuse to claim. It is the thing you shy over. It's the thing that you want to say nothing about, but says everything about you. Those parts are what should make someone love you, because those parts are the only thing that are truly real about you. Those parts are the reason you cry at sad songs. The reason you hate the smell of that cologne. The reason you prefer dogs over cats. The reason you never sleep at night. The reason you envy the relationship of close fathers and daughters. The reason you don't wear your natural hair. The reason you don't like to be touched. The reason you laugh when you're nervous. The reason for all that you do without reason. Those parts make you seem almost mad, insane if you will. But the one thing about those parts that you might never understand until you have hated yourself for too long is that; those parts are who you are.

I mean, loneliness scares me. There are times I only feel alone and that is no problem at all. I'm good in my own company, but being lonely is like… being the only person left on earth. It's like being in a dark room where there are no sources of lighting. It's complete darkness and the only escape from the emptiness is to close your eyes and when you do that, you open your mind to memories and the problem is, we can never choose which ones to think about. They choose us. I think loneliness chooses us too.

How to cry until you're dry

Go outside in the middle of the night
after the party goers have gone home
and before the birds sing their first song
Simmer in the darkness, that no longer
wreaks of paranoid looks over the shoulder.
You're by yourself; you're sure of it
Listen to your favorite song on replay in your head
feel your tears well up until you can't see through them
fight them back for a moment, then
remember there is no one around
let them hit the ground like bullets
cry over everything
cry over the things that still hurt
cry over the things that hurt
because they use to feel so good
Cry over your losses, cry over your victories
cry until crying just feels stupid
and your throat hurts, and you're just dry heaving
on your memories,
and your sorrows have no where left to drown
but make sure you cry loud when you do
hold nothing back
quiver your lip
feel weak in your limbs
Don't fear the night
as it echoes the sound
cry until you've set enough tears free
to float in and carry you home.

MIDNIGHT

stars are in your eyes
your skin blends into the night
you are where I dream

ABSTRALIA

My goosebumps rose
as the sun began to.
A faint chill wearing off
as the skies new warmth covered me,
as your warmth covered me.

You pulled me in
as your tired noises
were washed together
with the sounds
of the beach
and the sounds
of the birds
and the sounds
of the world waking up.

Your wine spritzed lips
kissed my skin

I was ready to do
the last 3 minutes
all over again.

WHEN YOU FALL OUT OF LOVE WITH ME

You will realize I am not all you thought I was. I often made stupid decisions. I jumped into most things blindly. I was a wreck, a disaster. My love was inconvenient and I was a nuisance. You will realize my smile was cracked. You will see scars that suddenly are so apparent. You will wonder how I got them. And because your love has faded, you will believe they were self-provoked.

You will see that I was either impatient or comatose. I had radical emotions and I never knew which way was up. I was all over the place. You now see that my sporadic bursts of energy, and the way I kept you on your toes was actually, so frustrating. You never knew what I wanted. You couldn't tell the difference from when I was happy or sad, because I acted all the same. Distant.

You will discover I wasn't articulate, I was a mind severely damaged by mental abuse. I was misunderstood and unique because I had gone insane. My heart was unattainable because there were so many pieces, you could not reach them all.

I wasn't an angel. In fact, maybe I was the devil in disguise. The devil most mischievous of all; the one who steals time. I've wasted yours, you'll realize – when you fall out of love with me.

I NEVER FINISH ANYTHING

I keep pushing things aside because I don't want things to happen at all if they aren't going to be right. I don't like the feeling of doing something and wishing I hadn't but I also never acknowledge that I too regret not doing things and wish I had. I wish I told you I loved you when it counted for something. I wish I had stood up for myself when you embarrassed me. I wish I had said yes to opportunities. I wish I didn't let myself cry in front of you. I wish I didn't stop trying. I wish I never doubted my abilities. I wish I didn't give up. I wish I never left. I wish I didn't run away from the good things that happened to me.. I wish I could finish something... anyth—

The only
Happy memory, that will
Ever be worth remembering is

Each
Night reality outranked my
Dreams.

I LOVE (PART II)

I love.. you still, your will, the way you fill the sky with stars, the way you don't seem as far as you are. The way you resonate with me like a good book that changes you internally. The kind that causes you to give life a second look, and a third, until you march to a new drum or word and you make a new path. And in saying that, I know the biggest worry about not being able to be present in someones life is constantly wondering if they will miss you, or forget you. I want you to know that I love how your memory reigns strong, how in your absence I notice the impact that is absent. I love that you were right, that this year went by quickly. I love that everything I'm doing, everything I'm achieving is something I'm so excited to share with you. I love how even without you being here I've forced myself to be strong because I know that's what you would have advised me. I don't like missing you but I love when I think that your life is going to be everything and more when you're back. I love your face, all of that. I love how when I try to locate, not analyze, my feelings about our friendship that it's everywhere – like you. Like your word. Like the changes in me. Like my confidence. Like the strokes in my art. Like my attentive posture. Like the dissolved shake in my voice. Like every tear I cry instead of quitting. Like every laugh I chuckle genuinely. Like every sincere thing I do even when I'm in a shit mood. You think I'm a good person and I say I'm good because of you and it's like the first time we spoke that destiny already was humming it's own tune – and then it happened. I changed. I was who being with you made me. I was becoming who I wanted to be; pieces of you, pieces of me, pieces of who you thought I was, pieces of who I dreamed and pieces that aren't in pieces. There's nothing about us that I would change, I was a plant and you watered me and on days I gave up I went thirsty to teach me I can't flourish like that. I can't grow if I don't want to try, if I don't think my life is valuable, if I don't think *I'm* valuable. You showed me I'm a rose, beautiful from far but a scar to those who get too close. But with bandaged fingers and brave intentions you held me when I needed it despite the consequences. That is why I am strong even only in your memory, even only until you return. You're the greatest thing to happen to me and because of that gift you gave to me I can be the greatest thing to someone else. I can give what you gave. I think I have somedays. I hope I am always; a reason, a season, a lesson and a blessing. I want to be each one.

Made in the USA
Charleston, SC
24 April 2014